North Leitrim Glens

*Strolls and Hill Walks in
North Leitrim & Sligo*

First published in Ireland by Shanksmare Publications
& North Leitrim Glens Development Co. Ltd.
© David Herman, 1993

ISBN - 0 9514547 2 2

Sketches: Michael Bussmann
Cover Photography: Jim McMorrow - Glencar
Sketch Maps: David Herman
Typing: Mary Fox
Project Co-ordinator: Jim McMorrow.
Assisted by : John Kennedy, Noel Loughlin.
Typeset by Drumlin Publications Ltd, Manorhamilton, Co. Leitrim
Printed by Colour Books, Dublin

Maps are based on the Ordnance Survey by permission of the Government of
Ireland (Permit No. 5659) and the Government of Northern Ireland
(Permit No. 549)

Shanksmare Publications
North Leitrim Glens Development Co. Ltd. Manorhamilton,
Co Leitrim. Tel: 072 - 55833

ACKNOWLEDGMENTS

I would like to thank all the kind people of North Leitrim and Sligo, and especially the people of Manorhamilton, who pointed out to me, a comparative stranger, a lot of routes in this book and who helped in a variety of ways to make my wife Mairin and myself feel at home and welcome.

In particular I should mention Gillian and Jim McMorrow of Manorhamilton and Aileen and Bill Hallowes of Dromahair for their hospitality and unstinting interest and support. I also thank Michael Purcell of the Geological Survey in Dublin and Tom Hobson of Lissadell for the time they both so willing gave me.

As always Mairin was my faithful and trusting companion on nearly all the walks, sometimes taking trust to the point of recklessness! She also provided the apt quotations from the works of W.B. Yeats which enhance my more mundane route descriptions.

I should emphasise that although this book is funded by the North Leitrim Glens Development Co. Ltd. the opinions expressed (good, bad and indifferent) are entirely my own.

THE AUTHOR

DAVID HERMAN was formerly a professional engineer with the Irish Electricity Supply Board. He has spent many years exploring the mountains of Ireland and has written extensively on them. He has walked farther afield, in Great Britain, the Alps, Greece, Spain, Malawi and the Himalayas. His last book was 'Great Walks Ireland' which was published in 1991 by Ward Lock of London.

Symbols used on Sketch Maps

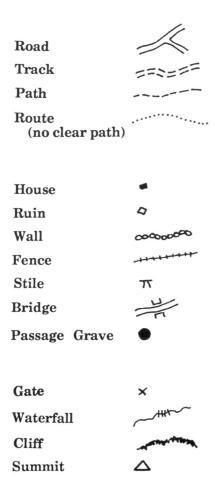

Road

Track

Path

Route
(no clear path)

House

Ruin

Wall

Fence

Stile

Bridge

Passage Grave

Gate

Waterfall

Cliff

Summit

On both OS and sketch maps the route is shown by a solid red line and the possible route(s) to the start by car shown by a dashed red line.

CONTENTS AND KEY MAP

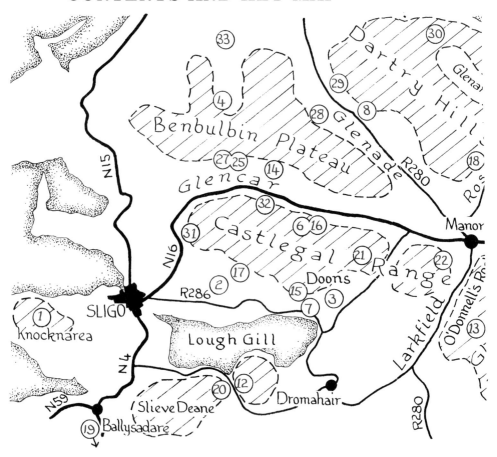

Introduction

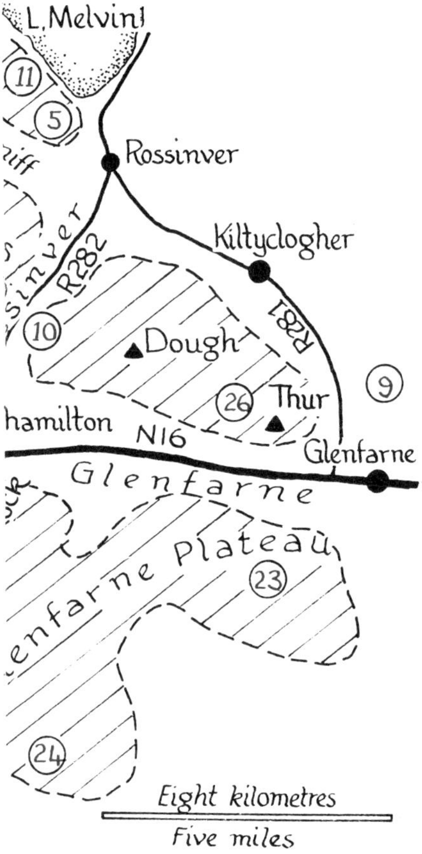

The Walks

L.Melvin

⑪

⑤

Rossinver

Kiltyclogher

⑩

▲Dough

㉖ Thur ⑨

hamilton N16

Glenfarne

Glenfarne

Glenfarne Plateau

㉓

㉔

Eight kilometres
Five miles

Walks with variations

Welcome!

The tourist brochures claim that *'Leitrim is Lovely'* and that *'Sligo is Surprising'*. Leaving alliteration aside we think we can combine these two phrases into one especially applicable to the hills, plateaus and the other wild places of North Leitrim and Sligo: *"(North) Leitrim and Sligo are Surprisingly Lovely"*.

With the publication of new maps for walkers a whole new dimension now awaits the discerning visitor: to explore the whole region at leisure, to reach its wild and remote places, to experience it through walking rather than to glimpse it through a car window.

This book contains full details of 33 walks in the uplands and quiet lowlands of North Leitrim and Sligo, ranging from strolls on rural roads to hard mountain treks. Each walk description gives full details of all you should know to make it as enjoyable and safe as possible: the terrain, transport, background information and of course full details of the route.

If you come initially for the easy strolls we hope you will go on to try some of the harder and more remote walks. Even if you are used only to walking on roads and tracks we think you will be delighted at the successful completion of a walk in which map and compass (and this book of course) were your only guides across trackless country.

So....... a warm welcome to the walking pleasures of North Leitrim and Sligo. We think - we *know* - you will not be disappointed.

HOW TO USE THIS BOOK

The 33 routes in the book are arranged roughly in order of difficulty; the short and easy ones at the start and the strenuous ones that normally require the use of map and compass and the wearing of suitable mountain gear towards the end. But please note that some routes have variations so that you may find just the route you are looking for under the heading of a harder (usually) or easier route. Look carefully at the list of routes before concluding that the walk you really want is not to be found.

The Ordnance Survey (OS) extracts (on a scale of 1:50000 - $1^1/_4$ inches to the mile) or the sketch maps (on a scale of 1:25000 - $2^1/_2$ inches to the mile) given with most route descriptions are sufficient cartographic help for the easier routes and some of the harder routes in good weather. However for the harder routes, and especially in poor visibility an OS map is essential. If in doubt – carry a map! The most appropriate OS map is specified in most route descriptions. *The symbols used are explained on page 5 of the book* . All the maps in this book are conventionally oriented, that is north towards the top of the page. There is more about maps on page 15.

Each route description is given in a fixed format, shortened where appropriate, and the following paragraphs try to explain any difficult or esoteric points which may arise in the course of that description.

We start, for at least some walks anyway, with a bit of culture! Some walk descriptions are preceded by a suitable quotation from the works of W.B. Yeats, Ireland's national poet, who drew heavily on this region in his writings.

A *Walking Time* is given in each route description. This is based on a speed of 4kph (about 2.5mph) on the flat with an additional hour allowed for every 500m (about 1650 ft) climbed. This allows time for short stops but not longer ones for example for food. Additional time is allowed for difficult terrain, steep descents etc. After a few walks you may decide that these times are wildly out. If this happens we can only suggest that you make the necessary adjustment using the distance and climb figures also given under the heading 'Walking Time'. Note that the climb figure is the cumulative climb and not the highest point reached. To give an example: if you start at 100m, climb to 600m, drop to 400m, climb again to 700m and return downhill all the way to the start, then the cumulative climb is 500m + 300m = 800m, not 700m, which is the highest point reached.

The definitive start of each walk (and a few other locations) is given under the heading *Transport* and uses a system of grid references taking the form GR 123456. Grid references locate any point on the map to the nearest hundred metres. A full explanation of this useful system is given in the margin of any small-scale map.

Unless the weather is fine and settled you should assume that a route for which a map is recommended also requires a compass – as well of course as the ability to use both. There are also specific notes under the heading *Navigational Difficulties*. Nonetheless it is most important to remember that a route that in good weather seems to have negligible navigational difficulties might turn out to have quite daunting ones in bad. This applies particularly to routes which are partly or wholly off tracks or paths.

Walking boots are recommended for the harder walks; under the heading *Terrain* you will find additional information which will help you choose suitable footwear. It is hard to be specific about which routes definitely need walking boots as a lot depends on the amount of rain in the days before your walk. If in doubt wear them.

As you walk each route check your progress against the route description and the map. Here and there we have indicated where small but unmistakable landmarks may be found, a sheep fold or a standing stone for instance. These might help to reassure that you are on the correct route or to pick up the route once again if you have temporarily lost it.

Distances and heights are taken from the Ordnance Survey 1:50000 maps and are given with various degrees of approximation depending on the context in which they are being used. For instance a distance along a road when one is driving may, if necessary, be expressed in tenths of miles (cars generally have milometers) whereas when one is walking an approximation to a half-mile might be more appropriate.

Both metric and imperial units have been used throughout. For heights this has led to seeming inconsistencies because these heights where available are taken directly from the metric and imperial Ordnance Survey maps. Thus Benbulbin's height is given as 526m and 1730ft, heights which do not exactly correspond mathematically but are those given on the 1:50000 (metric) and half-inch to the mile maps (imperial) respectively. This convention aids recognition on the maps. If only one height is available from the map then the other is a direct equivalent.

The unwary visitor may be puzzled by the fact that so many place names are spelt in a variety of ways on signposts and in books, maps and guides.

10

Be assured though that Benbulbin, Ben Bulbin, Benbulben and all the other versions of this place name refer to the one location and the same goes for the slightly different similar versions of other names. The versions used in this book are the same as on the Ordnance Survey 1:50000 maps and if none appears on them the most popular locally-used name is taken instead. Unfortunately the names of the mountain ranges and uplands do not appear at all on these maps and worse still, in some cases, there seems to be no local agreement as to their names. We have therefore taken the slight liberty of using locally-common versions which will be used consistently if not with the complete authority. The next section introduces the names of these ranges and the areas to which they refer.

AN OVERVIEW

The simplest way to consider the mountains of the region is to think of them as slices of a large cake, with a diameter of about 20km/12miles, whose sunken centre is at the town of Manorhamilton. (See the key map on pages 6 and 7.) We start therefore at the valley of *Glencar* between Sligo and Manorhamilton, and work our way clockwise through all the valleys and ranges. Glencar, with its small and attractive lake and towering lateral mountains is probably the most lovely valley in the entire region. An unusual geological feature of this valley and of Glenade (to be considered shortly) are the slumped hummocks that have fallen away from the plateau above and lie now in bizarrely shaped mounds on the valley sides.

Northwards the great gullied wall of the well-known *Benbulbin Plateau* overlooks the valley. This contains the highest point in the entire region though it reaches only a modest 647m/2120ft. A considerable stretch of the plateau edge drops sheer in formidable cliffs to glen and coastal plain. These cliffs guard an undulating moorland which sinks westward to expire in the lowlands near Manorhamilton.

North-east of the Benbulbin Plateau lies another lovely valley, *Glenade*, smaller and less well-known than Glencar but otherwise quite similar in views and beauty. To its north-east is another plateau, the *Dartry Hills,* like Benbulbin partly girded by sheer cliffs. Like it, it subsides towards Manorhamilton and like it, its highest point Arroo (523m/1712ft) is at its northern edge. However, it is considerably more undulating than Benbulbin with comparatively high ground at its centre and it is breached by a considerable valley, *Glenaniff,* one of the few that does not radiate from Manorhamilton.

The valley of *Rossinver* lies south-east of Dartry and eastward again is fairly forested country, the first such in this overview. This rises to distinct if rounded summits around *Dough* and to a fine north-facing escarpment at *Thur*, the highest point at 442m/1425ft. This whole area offers shorter and less demanding walks than those so far considered.

South of Dough and Thur runs the east-west valley of *Glenfarne* and south of it is a large remote lake-studded plateau rising to nearly 450m/1476 ft, which for want of a generally accepted name we call the *Glenfarne Plateau*. It is a little wetter underfoot than those farther west because it is not limestone and it has considerable afforestation on its steeply falling western flank. The *O'Donnell's Rock* area abuts this plateau, its north-west facing escarpment falling steeply to *Larkfield*, the valley running south-west from Manorhamilton. All this area offers shorter walks and is also of considerable archaeological (including industrial archaeological) interest.

The last 'slice' is that of the *Castlegal Range*, between Larkfield and Glencar, where we started this round. The Castlegal Range might be said to come from a different 'cake'. With bold, rocky and distinctive summits bounded by steep cliffs of varied heights this is the finest and most demanding walking country of the lot, so that its modest height (it rises to only 463m/1527ft) gives little indication of its grandeur. The *Doons*, a strange place of small flat-topped hills is a sub-area of Castlegal. Nor should we forget to mention probably the best-known of all this varied area's attractions: Lough Gill, which lies to the south of the Castlegal Range and greatly adds to its charms.

Lastly a few 'crumbs' which do not fit into the neat pattern outlined above. We will include walks in the *Slieve Deane* area south of Lough Gill, on well-known *Knocknarea* and in the archaeological treasure house of *Carrowkeel* far to the south. As we shall see, a few tasty morsels.

DOWN TO EARTH – A ROCKY FRAMEWORK

At this stage we will consider the geology of the region only in the briefest of terms, leaving most of the explanation to notes in the route descriptions as we encounter interesting features.

Let us continue with our cake analogy, but for geological purposes we will have to consider 'layers' rather than 'slices', with the oldest 'layer' at the bottom.

Starting with the lowest and oldest layer we have middle carboniferous limestone in the lowlands, followed in turn by upper carboniferous limestone,Yoredale sandstones and millstone grits, the latter three forming the higher ground. All these rocks are sedimentary, that is they are composed mostly of the shells of small and primitive animals and of deltaic deposits laid down about 350 million years ago.

It would be reasonable to assume that erosion, exposing layer after layer in turn, would mean that the least eroded and therefore the highest land would now have the youngest rocks in the whole region exposed while the foothills, the most eroded, would expose the oldest. This is only partly true. Since the time that the deposits were laid down there have been vertical movements of part of the region relative to other parts, so that the youngest rock (sandstones and grits) are exposed in the hills of the east and the older rocks (upper carboniferous limestone) are more exposed in the hills of the west, which are in fact somewhat higher than those farther east.

Let us stay for a couple of paragraphs with the carboniferous limestone since in the west and north of our region it forms some of its most spectacular scenery. Most of these rock strata were formed at the bottom of a sea in the Palaeozoic Era about 350 million years ago. Age after age small sea creatures fell to the sea floor and it is their remains, subsequently uplifted above sea-level and now mostly covered by bog that form the plateaus which are such a prominent feature of the area today.

Since limestone is highly soluble, water easily cuts down into it or percolates through it. Hence, where the limestone is exposed we find magnificent gullies where streams have cut a deep channel in the limestone in their efforts to descend from the plateau to the plain. Water also sinks down through the cracks in the limestone and subsequently enlarges these thus forming swallow holes (some a few metres across). The water has in some cases made a passage right down through the limestone and forms underground streams which emerge at the foot of the limestone cliffs.

Between the younger uplands of the east and the older ones of the west is a long narrow tail of metamorphic rocks which dates from very roughly 600 million years ago. These are totally different and much older rocks than any yet considered. The tail stretches all the way from the Ox Mountains to the west of our region, north-east along the southern shore of Lough Gill and finally, north-east of its last peak Benbo, peters out near Manorhamilton.

Lastly, we must mention glacial action, which took place only thousands of years ago, a mere eye-blink in geological terms. This sharpened the existing river valleys, changing their original shallow V-profile to a U and giving us the lovely glens such as Glencar and Glenade that are such an attractive feature of the region.

TRANSPORT

Access to the Region

Four national primary routes converge on Sligo town, the N15 from Donegal and Derry, the N16 from Enniskillen and Belfast through Manorhamilton, the N4 from Dublin and the N17 from Galway. A national secondary route, the N59 is routed from Ballina through Ballysadare, which is just south of Sligo.

A rail service links Dublin through Collooney and Carrick-on-Shannon to Sligo and there is an airport in Sligo with regular flights to Dublin.

Express bus services run by Irish Bus/Bus Eireann also converge on Sligo with services from Derry, Belfast, Dublin, Athlone and beyond, Galway, Achill and Ballina.

Access by road within the Region

While there is quite a complex network of roads within the region, quality does not always match quantity. Signposting is also indifferent so it is advisable to take a small-scale map to find your way on country roads.

The road system may be studied on any road map, so there is little point in duplicating the information here. However, we may note that the Benbulbin Plateau, the Castlegal Range and the mountains east of Manorhamilton are well served by the N16 and the smaller roads which lead off it and that the R280 through Glenade is close to both the Benbulbin Plateau and the Dartry Hills. Note also that there is a particularly complex network of useful roads south of the Castlegal Range.

Bus Services within the Region

Irish Bus/Bus Eireann run the local bus services (that is those that will stop anywhere as long as it is safe to do so). It can be quite difficult for the uninitiated to follow the timetable because it uses local names which do not appear on the maps. Nearby bus services are noted under the heading *Transport* in the route descriptions but it is essential to check the timetable and advisable to confirm it by ringing the local bus office

14

before you travel. The timetable numbers given in the route descriptions are just that - the buses themselves do not have numbers.

The service given in any one table can vary in timing and route depending on the day of the week. Nearly all the infrequent services run *towards* Sligo in the morning and *outwards* in the evening so that Sligo is not a good centre for those relying solely on buses. Note also that none of the infrequent services run on Sundays.

The express services, because they stop only at selected places are of little use within the region. However those routes east from Sligo through Manorhamilton, Glenfarne and Blacklion may be useful for accessing the mountains near these towns.

MAPS

No fewer than four 1:50000 (1 1/4 inches to the mile) maps between them cover the region. While there is some overlap between the sheets the difficulty with this plentitude is that a few routes are on the edge or even the corner of a map. It is therefore fortunate that, as explained in an earlier section a map is not essential for walking some of the routes; in any case most of the routes described are on the one sheet (sheet 16).

Two of these maps are in the Republic of Ireland series, two in Northern Ireland's, with the more useful maps being the Republic's because they cover the bulk of the mountain area. (In the following description the terms *northern* and *southern* refer to the Northern Ireland and Republic of Ireland series respectively and have no geographical connotation.) There are some stylistic differences between the two (e.g. the northern series is coloured and the southern is not) but the main difference is that the northern series shows cliffs by symbols - and errs on the side of caution - whereas the southern shows them only by the convergence of contour lines, leaving the reader to judge exactly where they are.

Let's look at the individual sheets. Sheet 16 (southern series) covers Manorhamilton and the area to the north-west of it (precisely its south-eastern corner is 9km/6 miles south-east of the town). As we have already said it covers the bulk of the routes. Sheet 25 (also southern series) covers the area south-west of Manorhamilton, its north-east corner being very close to the town. The Northern Ireland sheets cover roughly the area to the east of Manorhamilton, sheet 17 to the north-east and sheet 26 to the south-east.

The half-inch to the mile (1:126720) maps might be useful for travel by car especially on minor roads. Only the southern series of the half-inch maps is now published, the relevant one for this region being sheet 7. The equivalent sheet of the northern series, sheet 3, is much the better and should be used if still available.

SAFETY

There is a broad spectrum of walking to be had between the poles of timidity and foolhardiness and its exact width depends on your ability and experience, on the route you propose to follow and, most important, on the conditions on the day.

Please read the general notes given under 'How to Use this Book' especially those under the headings 'Walking Time', 'Terrain' and 'Navigational Difficulties'. Next read the specific notes under these headings in the route description of the walk you propose. If it is one of the harder walks take a careful note of the weather forecast, remembering that the higher you are the greater the likelihood of reduced visibility. Do not attempt a walk very much beyond your present experience level unless the weather is fine and settled and likely to remain so. Do not walk alone: on the harder walks there should be at least three in a walking party, so that if one person is injured the second can stay with him/her and the third go for help.

Dress for the occasion; walking boots with ankle support, raingear and an additional pullover are recommended for the harder walks. Take sufficient food and a flask. Do not, however take so much that you are weighed down with unnecessary clutter. A rucksack is highly recommended as it leaves the hands free.

On the walk keep a close watch on your position on the map and on weather changes and turn back if worsening weather justifies it. Remember that bad visibility can very easily disorient and chill you and turn what would otherwise be an easy stroll into a very frightening experience. Do not press on regardless.

When you are satisfied that you have taken all reasonable precautions get out into the mountains, use a bit of common sense and most important - enjoy yourself!

RIGHT OF WAY AND GOOD BEHAVIOUR

Ireland does not have a cast-iron system of rights of way so that unless you are on a recognised way or in State forest the owner of the land you are walking on is within his/her rights to tell you to clear off. If this happens - go!

However, in practice farmers and other landowners are trusting folk and will allow you to wander freely. Do not betray their trust. Act as if you were an uninvited guest on other peoples' property, because that is exactly what you are. A few specifics: do not allow dogs to roam free over sheep-grazing land, that is nearly the whole of the uplands. Do not stand on fence strands: you can always find a spot at which to cross without doing so. The strands may look the same afterwards but they will have been permanently damaged. Leave gates as you found them, open or closed, and if you have to climb one do so at the hinged end. And lastly, never, never litter in the country - or anywhere else for that matter.

THE LEITRIM WAY

The Leitrim Way/Slí Liatroma is at present the only long distance waymarked route in the region. Its northern end is at Manorhamilton and from there it runs south into the O'Donnell's Rock area, where there is a branch, the O'Donnell's Rock Way, which returns to Manorhamilton. The main route runs east and south again to cross the Glenfarne Plateau, thereafter descending into the town of Dowra. Passing out of the region covered by this book it continues south along the eastern side of Lough Allen to end up in Drumshanbo. The route as far as Dowra is almost all side road and track, much of it through remote upland country.

The total distance from Manorhamilton to Dowra is about 24km/15miles and the length of the O'Donnell's Rock branch is about 9km/6miles. The northern end of the route is shown on 1:50000 sheet 16, but the remainder is not shown on the maps.

Walk 1   Knocknarea

Came to the cairn-heaped grassy hill
Where passionate Maeve is stony-still"
(The Wanderings of Oisin)

Everyone (well, almost everyone) visiting Sligo climbs Knocknarea. A huge cowpat topped by a massive passage grave, its distinctive shape is visible for miles around. Conversely, its top gives excellent views of coastline, plain and near and not so near hills. It scarcely needs a description but that given here at least recommends a different downward route to the upward.

Walking Time: In spite of a nearby signpost's (and several authorities') assertion that it takes three-quarters of an hour for the ascent alone, the path is clear and underfoot conditions easy so the whole walk should scarcely take an hour. For the record the distance is 4km/2.5miles and the climb 220m/700ft.

Transport: Take John Street and Upper John Street west out of Sligo, continue straight through a crossroads after about 3 miles (and so signposted back to Sligo), take the first turn right (signposted) and park in the carpark a short distance up. The bus in table 285 may also be taken.

Map: None needed, but take 1:50000 sheet 25 or a half-inch map, if you have either, to identify peaks.

Terrain and Navigational Difficulties: None.

Route: Simplicity itself. Take the neatly paved path from the carpark up to a copse, swing left here directly uphill, cross a gigantic iron stile and climb quite steeply from there to the top of Knocknarea (327m/1078ft, *Cnoc na Rí*, 'the hill of Kings')[1]. For the descent go to the west (that is, the far) side of the passage grave and there take the rightmost of two clear paths, that with the partly ruined wall on its left. Where it cravenly bends right to shirk a precipitous cliff ahead, follow it equally cravenly, to and along a forest border on the left. Swing right away from the forest to cross the stile again, and walk back to the start.

Note

1. The huge cairn of stones on the summit, 10m/30ft high and 180m/600ft in circumference is the reputed burial place of Queen Maev of Connaught, who reigned in the first century AD. However, it is more likely that she is buried elsewhere.

Knocknarea

Walk 2   Deerpark

"The woods were round them, and the yellow leaves
Fell like faint meteors in the gloom..."

(Ephemera)

A stroll,mostly through mature forest to impressive court cairns.

Walking Time: A leisurely half-hour.

Transport: The starting point at GR 756372 is a few hundred metres west (that is nearer Sligo) of the signpost for Keelogyboy (route 14). The court cairns are signposted from the road.

Terrain and Navigational Difficulties: Tracks and paths all the way.

Map: A road map or half-inch map might be useful to find the start, but none is required for the walk itself.

Route: The route to the cairns is signposted with admirable economy of effort: a mute arrow points upwards to the right from the initial forest track. The cairns[1] crown the top of a hill from which any remaining views are fast disappearing under a rising tide of conifers.

For the return continue onwards along the outward path, turn left at the stone wall (no other direction is feasible) along which there are good views over fields to Colgagh Lough[2], the only wide views on the walk. Swing left on the path where the wall turns right and turn left slightly upward where it meets a forest track. Continue through pleasant forest back to the start.

Notes

1. This is one of the finest court cairns in Ireland. The central court is 15m/50ft long and oval-shaped. Two burial chambers open off at one end, and one at the other. It was built in the 3rd millenium BC.

   There is another theory about the possible use of these edifices. A Victorian cleric, noting that the opes into the side chambers were too low for humans, concluded that they must therefore be for small animals. He therefore suggested that the site was used for animal-baiting, the side chambers for the opposing animals, the central chamber for the combat between them.

2 Colgagh Lough is a hydrological oddity in that it has no surface connection with another lake or the sea. As it lies on limestone rock, which easily allows the formation of underground passages, there must be such a passage connecting it with Lough Gill.

Walk 3   O'Rourkes Table

A very short walk to a flat-topped hill between Dromahair and Manorhamilton, where with little physical effort, excellent views of Lough Gill and the nearby Castlegal Range, as well as farther away hills may be had.

Walking Time: About a quarter of an hour each way. The distance to the top is only a few hundred metres and the climb about 100m/350ft.

Transport: The start is from the Dromahair to Manorhamilton road (R286) at GR 809350. From Parke's Castle on the northern shore of Lough Gill drive east, take the turn left signposted 'Manorhamilton $8^1/_2$', turn left at the first crossroads and watch out for the sign on the left bearing the curious legend 'Tabla Ui Ruairc Scene of the Valley lay Smiling Moore's Famous Melody for which a tentative explanation is offered below.[1] If coming from the Manorhamilton direction watch out for a church on the right. The start is a few hundred metres farther on.

Map: None except perhaps a road map needed, but take a half-inch map if you have one for identifying nearby peaks (O'Rourkes Table falls close to the borders of 1:50000 sheets 16, 25 and 26 thus preventing easy all-round identification unless you use all these maps). O'Rourkes Table is called by the townland name Doonmorgan on sheets 16 and 25 but by the name given here on sheet 26.

Terrain and Navigational Difficulties: Some rough terrain but the short distance of the whole route means that it is of no great significance. No navigational difficulties.

Route: Very simple. Follow the sign along the side of a garden, through a gate, and turn left to pick up a track. Where the track peters out turn right uphill, go through a gap in a wall to enter a steep-sided pass with O'Rourkes Table on the right, its limestone cliffs partly smothered in ivy. Ascend the west side of the Table (that is at the far end of the pass) by crossing a stile and scrambling up the path beyond it. [2]

The Table give excellent views with the eastern end of the Castlegal Range worthy of study, especially if you intend to climb it later. Return by the same route.

Notes

1. Signposts in this area try to tell the whole story and not merely indicate direction. In this instance a little punctuation would help, yielding 'Tabla Ui Ruairc (ie O'Rourkes Table): Scene of "The Valley Lay Smiling", Moore's famous melody'. Thomas Moore, the early 19th century lyricist, wrote the words of a song about O'Rourke's wife Dervorgilla, who in the 12th century was spirited away by Dermot MacMurrough. Subsequently the mourning O'Rourke takes himself up to the Table to lament.

2. The Table top is dome-shaped and appears therfore to be a tiny raised bog. The vegetation on the top, heathers and bilberries, would tend to confirm this. Near the north-east corner is a swallow hole of great but unmeasured depth. It is called, in a mixture of Gaelic and onomatopoeia, *Poll a Ding Dong*. 'Poll' means a hole, and 'ding dong' is the sound made by a stone as it hits the hole's side after being thrown into it.

   William Bulfin, the early 20th century cyclist and wanderer waxed eloquent about the Table. The reference to lengths in the first sentence seems grossly exaggerated: *"The table is about two miles long and half a mile in width. And such a royal tablecloth! Rich, fragrant, clustering heather! The top of the mountain is covered with peat, and the peat is covered with a growth of heather in which you stand waist high. Rank, sedgy grass and heaps of moss and huge tufts of mountain fern are along the edge near the wood, and right in the centre... there is moss in which you sink to your knees".*

21

Walk 4   Upper Gleniff

It is possible but not very profitable to do a circuit by road of Gleniff. This much shorter version encompasses as much variety as the full circuit and gives excellent close-up views of the varied terrain which is such an interesting feature of the valley.

Walking Time: Distance 3km/2miles, climb 80m/250ft, walking time 1hr.

Transport: By car to Ballaghnatrillick (GR 737502). Here you should stop for a moment to examine the extraordinary profile of Benwiskin to the south-west. Continue by car into Gleniff, taking the road *not* signposted 'Yeats Country Drive'. Park at the shed on the right (GR 731477) just after the end of forest 1.8 miles farther on.

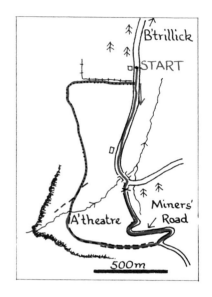

Map: None needed.

Terrain and Navigational Difficulties: Mostly road and path, but also some wet ground at the end. No navigational difficulties.

Route: Walk into the valley a further 800m/half-mile, taking here the gravelled miners' road on the right from which there are increasingly good views across the valley and beyond it to the encircling hills. After about 800m/half mile, take a grassy track right that has a high stone wall embankment on its left (upper side).

This track takes you around the rim of a large smoothly-sloped amphitheatre on the right, with rocky crags up to the left split by a wide vertical cut. This cut is in turn topped by an upper basin gouged out of the highest point of the encircling hills [1, 2]. At the point where the stream issuing from this cut crosses what is now a vestigial path take another path which you will see ahead running diagonally downhill to the right.

Where this levels out branch pathlessly left off it to traverse grassy hummocky ground below the slopes on the left, from which a large cave entrance [3] may be seen. Continue to the end of the hummocks and descend right over wet ground (alas!) with a fence on the left. Cross the fence onto the road and turn left for the start.

22

Notes

1. The cable crossed here belongs to an early stage in the mine's history and formed part of an aerial railway which ran from near the old school, the large abandoned building near here. It was used in the barytes mining further to the south.

   There are notes on the mining itself under walk 33.

2. The upper basin seems to be a collapsed cave, whose floor and walls are intact.

3. From here the cave system, called Diarmuid and Grainne's Bed, is about 250m/800ft above and involves a climb over grass and a rock scramble. Diarmuid and Grainne, a legendary couple from Ireland's heroic era had many odd lodging places throughout the length and breadth of the land.

   From the entrance chamber visible from here are three caves, a large centre one and two side chambers. Because of the severe erosion on the steep slopes up to the caves a visit is not recommended.

   The cave has been truncated. During one of the ice ages a glacier, advancing down Gleniff, sheared off part of the cave system here leaving the present entrance which had hitherto been tucked away in the heart of the mountain.

Walk 5   Near Parke's Castle

A short but energetic stroll steeply up through a mixed wood and along a narrow, turbulent stream. There are good views over Lough Gill and part of the flat-topped hills of the Doon country.

Walking time: A leisurely half-hour or so.

Transport: From Parke's Castle on the north shore of Lough Gill drive east (ie with the Castle on the right) along the R286 taking the first turn left after 0.3 miles. If travelling west turn right at the phone kiosk on the left within sight of the Castle. Park in the forest carpark on the left a few metres farther on (GR 787352).

Terrain and Navigational Difficulties: None - path all the way, with only one decision point.

Map: None needed either for the route or the journey to the start (the Castle is well signposted).

Route: Take the path from the carpark and branch right a few metres farther on thus facing the climb at the start rather than at the end. Do not despair - there are two seats at crucial points on the climb and at the second of these you can climb over the wall (carefully please!) to enhance already wide views. For the return drop steeply to the stream, crossing it twice on foot-bridges to reach the start.

Walk 6   Glenade: Sracleighreen

A short there-and-back walk all on track, giving widening views over Glenade Lough to the great walls of the Benbulbin Plateau and later the near cliffs of Keeloges. It ends on the edge of the Dartry moorland, a moorland slashed by the impressive gorges of two streams.

Walking Time: Distance 5km/3miles, climb 160m/500ft, walking time 1 hr 30 mins.

Transport: The starting point proper is north of Glenade Lough on the R280 at GR 815476. However, since parking is hazardous there it might be better to start at Glenade post office, a few hundred metres north-east along the R280.

Route: Take the gated track on the left (left coming from the post office, that is) - it's just before a small wood - and follow it through two other gates thus rising increasingly high over Glenade, and then along the side of a narrow valley onto moorland. After the third gate you will see, far down on the right, the junction of two streams which descend in impressive cascades and waterfalls. You can scramble down around here and find lovely places to explore along the banks. Don't forget that arduous climb back to the track!

Walk 7   Rossinver Waterfalls

The Glenaniff River enters Lough Melvin near Rossinver and near its end it descends to the lake in a series of delightful waterfalls flowing over limestone slabs in a tiny wooded valley. A riverside path has been laid out here and it makes a pleasant quarter hour or so to walk it. There are plans to extend the path downstream to Lough Melvin.

Transport: The walk is signposted from Rossinver and begins about 2km/1mile west of the village at GR 913480.

Pinnacle Gully

Walk 8   Glencar :   Gleneigh

Gleneigh, a short but comparatively shallow and broad valley, is tucked into the northern slopes of the Castlegal Range, between Hangman's Hill and Leean. Both its forest tracks, which service burgeoning plantations and its old secluded roads, which reach now mostly abandoned farms, alike offer scope for this short, scenic and navigationally easy walk.

Walking Time: Distance 4km/2.5miles, climb 130m/430ft, walking time 1 hr 15 mins.

Transport: If coming from Sligo pass the end of Glencar Lough and turn right just pass the school on the left about 2 miles further on. If coming from Manorhamilton turn left 0.6 miles past the statue on the right. In either case park after 0.6 miles at the second turn left (GR 792407).

Map: None needed.

Terrain and Navigational Difficulties: None.

Route: Easy. Take the left turn at the parking place, ignore the right fork just after the stream and continue up through some scattered and some not so scattered forest to the crossroads. Turn right here, initially slightly downhill, and continue high around the valley on an ancient narrow road, passing some upland houses, most sadly abandoned, some apparently not. Swing downhill where the new forest road heads up left (and is obviously not the route) and so return to the start. And here you may feel that you have earned a little rest, one which may be enhanced by choosing a sylvan site down by the stream you passed at the start.

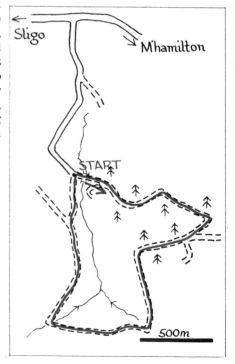

Walk 9   Glenfarne Forest

A pleasant, fairly short walk along the shores of wooded Upper Lough Macnean, returning through hilly agricultural land.

Walking Time: Distance 8km/5miles, climb 90m/300ft, walking time 2 hrs 15 mins.

Transport: Drive to the forest carpark (GR 024390) a mile or so north-east of Glenfarne. The park is signposted from the R281 (Kiltyclogher road).

Map: None needed and since both 1:50000 sheets 17 and 26 would have to be taken with consequence irritating cross-referencing you are probably better off with the composite version given here.

Terrain and Navigational Difficulties: None.

Route: Walk back along the forest track from the carpark, turn first right, ignore the turn left, cross the stream and turn right at the tee beyond it. Ignore the next right turn which would bring you onto a wooded peninsula and instead swing slightly left uphill so reaching the shore of the lake.

Continue along the shore to a minor road and turn sharply left onto it. Take it to its end at a tee, turn left and take the first turn left (it is just before a bridge and the track right makes the junction technically a crossroads). Walk straight ahead to the start.

Walk 10   Saddle Hill

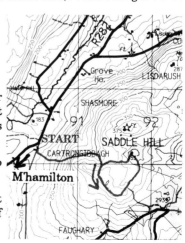

Saddle Hill overlooks the valley of Rossinver and the town of Manorhamilton. This short walk, barely more than an up-and-down, offers good views over a varied landscape.

Walking Time: Distance 3.5km/2miles, climb 200m/700ft, walking time 1 hr 15 mins.

Transport: Take the R282 (Rossinver road) out of Manorhamilton and park at the sharp turn-off right (at GR 904443) 3.4 miles along this road.

Upper Gleniff

Map: Take 1: 50000 sheets 16 or 17 if you have either, but they are not essential.

Terrain and Navigational Difficulties: Mostly track, some parts muddy; otherwise open country, some parts wet. No navigational difficulties.

Route: Walk a few metres along the side road and then take the rough track left up through fields and occasional rocky outcrops to a tee. Turn left here and follow it to its end near the southern top of Saddle Hill. Walk south-east along the summit ridge to Saddle Hill (unnamed on the O.S. map). Then head north to a forestry track and at a gate on the right leave it to walk north over rough ground to the main top of Saddle Hill (375m/1230ft), crowned by a ring fort. [1]

You will have noticed another track running nearer the main summit on the ascent and you should now head south to its end. However do not follow it for long because lower down it become a veritable sea of mud. Instead, when you see the track used on the ascent walk the short distance across open ground to it and follow it back to the start.

Notes

1. Although this well-formed circle is on a summit it is more likely to be a ring fort rather than a hill fort. The latter is usually much bigger and would have been a tribal meeting place and not a habitation. Ring forts were places where families lived permanently and were inhabited in a few cases until as late as the 18th century.

Walk 11   Lough Melvin: Sheenun

Sheenun is a bold promontory dominating a branch of the Dartry Hills between Glenaniff and the large expanse of Lough Melvin. Though not lofty its isolated location gives it a wide panorama, especially to the plains and lakeland to the north.

Walking Time: Distance 4km/2.5miles, climb 150m/500ft, walking time 1 hr 30 mins, including some time to cross fences.

Transport: Drive to Rossinver near the southern end of Lough Melvin and take the minor road west here (ie left from Manorhamilton direction). Turn right over the bridge after 1.4 miles, and take the second turn right (signed 'Barr road'). Drive for a further 1.1 miles and stop near a grassy track zig-zagging up the hillside on the left, (GR 911497). (If you drive as far as a dirt track heading *straight up* the hill you have gone a few hundred metres too far, but do not despair since this is an easier place to park.)

Map: 1:50000 sheet 16 or 17.

Terrain and Navigational Difficulties: The terrain is mostly heathery underfoot but generally not too wet. The main problem is fences: they run at close intervals and some are difficult to cross without damaging them. Please be careful (of yourself as well as them). There are no navigational difficulties.

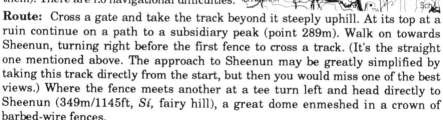

Route: Cross a gate and take the track beyond it steeply uphill. At its top at a ruin continue on a path to a subsidiary peak (point 289m). Walk on towards Sheenun, turning right before the first fence to cross a track. (It's the straight one mentioned above. The approach to Sheenun may be greatly simplified by taking this track directly from the start, but then you would miss one of the best views.) Where the fence meets another at a tee turn left and head directly to Sheenun (349m/1145ft, *Sí*, fairy hill), a great dome enmeshed in a crown of barbed-wire fences.

At the top you will be rewarded by a wide panorama. Contemplation of the gently shelving plain of wet bogland and lines of sturdy fence to the west should quickly convince you that further progress would be tortuous. Instead face north and head towards two plantations, keeping close to their left to pick up a track running beside a tiny reclusive stream. At the road turn right for the start, a walk of about 1.5km/1mile and offering good views across Lough Melvin .[1]

Notes

1. Ladder Farms: Long narrow townlands, divided into 'ladder farms', run up the higher slopes of Sheenun facing Lough Melvin. Farmhouses are located on steps within each strip, the houses at upper levels now mostly derelict.

Walk 12   Slish Wood

"Where dips the rocky highland
Of Sleuth Wood in the lake"   (The Stolen Child)

A pleasant lakeshore and hillside walk, tracks all the way. It has good views of Lough Gill, especially at the start.

Walking Time: Distance 3.5km/2miles, climb 110m/350ft, walking time 1 hr.

Transport: From Sligo take the N4 (Dublin road) turning left after about 2 miles towards Dromahair. Park in the carpark on the left, the second along this road, after a further 3.5 miles (at GR 739314).

Map: None needed.

Terrain and Navigational Difficulties: Easy to follow tracks all the way.

Route: Cross the forest bar at the north end of the carpark and walk along the track beyond with the lake and its tiny wooded islands glimpsed through lovely deciduous trees close on the left. After about 2km/1mile the track rises from the shore and at the first fork go right[1], so looping back into a recently felled area. Here the great rocks of Killerry on the left look temptingly near but the terrain to it is dreadfully difficult and better not attempted. Continue to the tee close to the carpark and turn left for it.

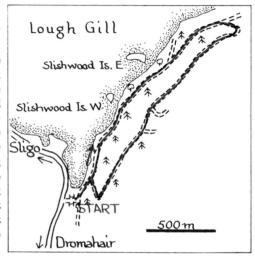

Notes

Yeats in Slish Wood: When Yeats was 22 or 23 he decided to spend the night in Slish Wood for 'mystical reasons', but could not sleep because he imagined that the ranger would evict him. For this reason and because this adventure involved a walk of 30 miles he arrived home exhausted. *"My uncle's general servant believed I had spent the night in a different fashion and invented the excuse to deceive my uncle, and would say to my great embarrassment, for I was prudish as an old maid, 'And you had a good right to be fatigued'."*

1.The area around here and especially those eastern-facing sides of hills that are clothed in oak woods are a perfect environment for rare butterflies. The Purple Hairstreak has its northmost station in Ireland among the oaks along the banks of a stream east of here. Other species in the area include Wood Whites, Dingy Skippers and Orange Tips in early summer, Meadow Browns and Ringlets in midsummer and small Tortiseshells, Peacocks and Red Admirals in late summer.

O'Donnell's Rock dominates the valley of Larkfield and is seen from there as a high ridge, old scrubland on the steep slopes and outcrops of limestone along the summit. Behind this ridge and of course not visible from Larkfield is a rather bleak moorland which stretches far across to the east. This easy walk samples all three terrain types and in addition gives good views west over Benbo and beyond to the Castlegal Range.

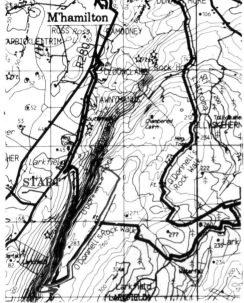

Walking Time: Distance 5.5km/ 3.5miles, climb 190m/600ft, walking time 1 hr 45 mins.

Transport: Take the R280 for 1.1 miles from the main crossroads in Manorhamilton, turning left here onto a minor road (unsigned). Turn left again onto a dirt track (signposted "O'Donnell's Rock") after 1.0 miles and park at the first hairpin bend (GR 883367).

Map: 1:50000 sheet 16 or 26, the former more useful to identify nearby peaks.

Terrain and Navigational Difficulties: A short stretch of boggy ground, but otherwise no difficulties.

Route: Walk up the track, so ascending through the scrubland of the escarpment on an easy, diagonal trajectory. Rounding the end of the ridge, ignore the turn right and face north into the moorland.

Walk straight ahead to the track's end facing a tiny rounded hill guarded by a high stone wall. Turn left at this wall and follow it (in parts it is bolstered or replaced by a fence or earth bank) gently downhill as far as the steep drop into Larkfield. Turn left here and walk the escarpment edge[1] following where convenient an intermittent path or stone wall, but do not descend right until the track is reached again. Turn right onto it for the start.

Notes

1. Traces of an old railway line, including a bridge may be seen in the valley of Larkfield. The line, which ran from Enniskillen through Manorhamilton to Sligo was built in the 1870s to stimulate iron and coal mining in the Leitrim area and to facilitate the carriage of cattle to the north-east. Never very profitable, it was dealt a body blow by civil strife in the 1920s and the disruption caused by the setting up of the international border. The line closed in 1957.

Stacks on King's Mountain

Walk 14 Keelogyboy

Keelogyboy is a large, easily accessible area of undulating plateau flanked in parts by fine scree-covered cliffs, and not a prize greyhound as the uninitiated might think from the name ('Keelogyboy' comes from *Cill Óga Buí,* 'the young yellow wood'). The views from it over Lough Gill and beyond towards Sligo town in the middle distance and the ranges beyond the town are excellent. An easy and rewarding walk.

Walking Time: Distance 4km/2.5miles, climb 270m/900ft (including the climb to the top of Keelogyboy), walking time 1hr 30 mins.

Transport: By car to a side road west of the mountain (GR 757386). Take the N16 from Sligo, branching right just outside the town onto the R286 and branch left shortly afterwards onto the Manorhamilton road. After 3.4 miles turn left steeply uphill at a signpost carrying the simple but reassuring legend 'Keelogyboy'. Ignore the right turn and park at the fork 0.9 miles up from the sign.

From the Manorhamilton direction take the N16, branch left onto the R286, after 3.6 miles branch right onto the Colgagh road and watch out for the Keelogyboy signpost after a further 3.8 miles.

The Saturday service of the table 282 bus might possibly be used for this walk.

Map: 1:50000 sheet 16 or 25.

Terrain and Navigational Difficulties: Mostly path but some high vegetation makes for heavy going. Apart from ensuring that you ascend and descend Keelogyboy by much the same route, no navigational problems.

Route: Take the right fork, so keeping forest on the left. Cross the first gate and turn right to head steadily upwards, initially on a track. From here the Keelogyboy plateau appears as three blocks, the centre one farther back and the right with characteristically knobbly outcrops on its left shoulder. (On the 1:50000 map these peaks appear as 438m, 434m, 417m left to right.)

Where the track peters out look for a path close to a fence on the right which is worth finding to avoid wading through high heather. At the fence corner take a last look at Lough Gill and continue, still on a path, into the narrow steep-sided pass ahead. At its highest point climb to the Keelogyboy summit (438m/1446ft) on the left, which has an unusual limestone rock field and commands excellent views. This ascent is just a there-and-back, but since Keelogyboy is a large and navigationally confusing plateau make sure of the 'and-back' by taking care to retrace your steps.

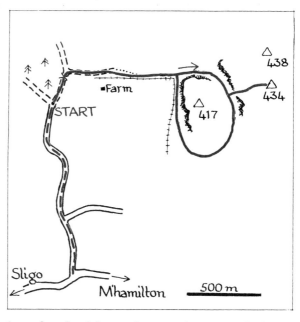

Back at the top of the pass continue down the other side to be confronted by a lake uncannily like Lough Gill, the one from which you were walking. Surprisingly it *is* Lough Gill. The explanation: the pass swings sharply right so that you do not reach the other side of the range but instead emerge on the same side. This mystery assimilated, contour right on a clear path on the left of which steep ground falls to two small lakes and a few tiny hillocks. Follow this path across several sections of scree where it is sometimes difficult to discern but soldiers on and provides a comparatively easy and safe route. Eventually the path descends to a fence. Keep it on the left as far as the corner thus rejoining the upward path. Turn left for the start and try to ensure that you make the difficult transition from path to track on the descent.

Walk 15   Glencar Waterfall

"Where the wandering water gushes
From the hills above Glen-Car,
in pools among the rushes
That scarce could bathe a star."   (The Stolen Child)

Like Niagara though on a rather smaller scale Glencar Waterfall is noted more for its breadth than its height, a modest 30m/100ft. The stream that supplies this fall rises high on the Benbulbin Plateau and a circuit round it (the stream, that is) gives a short but not all that easy introduction to an area which encompasses a wide diversity of scenery far and near. Be prepared for some rough terrain and a stiff climb, but you can also anticipate an ample reward for your efforts.

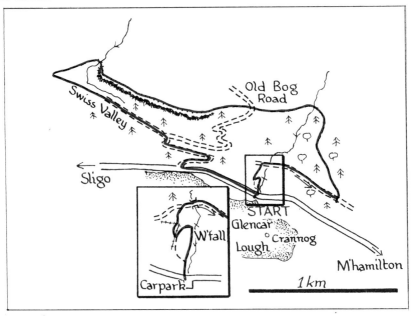

Walking Time: Distance 4.5km/3miles, climb 250m/800ft, walking time 2 hrs thus allowing about 15 mins over standard for a steep descent and a possibly difficult stream-crossing.

Transport: By car to the carpark at the eastern end of the north shore of Glencar Lough(GR 760434). The carpark, on the southern side of the road (right from Sligo) is well signposted. The table 282 bus service might also be used for this walk.

Map: Take 1:50000 sheet 16 if you have it.

Terrain and Navigational Difficulties: Mostly track or path, though some rough pathless terrain. Take care not to wander off the route where there is no forestry to guide you.

Route: Take the direct path to the waterfall and having admired it– and it *is* quite impressive[1]– start back towards the road on the upper path, the one farther from the stream. At its highest point, cross a broken fence right and walk up through the field beyond it to its nearest corner. In the forest beyond, ascend on a clear path to a track, turn right onto it and cross a rough wooden bridge.

The next part of the route requires some attention. Continue along the track for about five minutes, not allowing the lovely views of Glencar glimpsed through trees to distract you.[2] Where it levels off take a narrow secluded path on the left which slants back sharply uphill, following it through trees parallel to the fast-flowing stream on the left.

On the plateau continue on the path as it bends sharply left, trees now only on this side. Cross the narrow channel of the stream – and around here the path has all but disappeared - and walk round a tiny field set incongruously on the edge of the plateau. Cross another deep-set stream and a track (it's the Old Bog Road and there is plenty of bog on your right to justify the name). Here you can descend directly home but be advised that you will be missing the finest scenery of the route.

The next section reveals the walk's greatest delights: the hills of Castlegal across Glencar and the cliffs and steep ground on the near side of the valley, set off by occasional sorties of trees penetrating into high rocky ground. Keep forest on the left and at its end follow an earth bank uphill, with steep ground on the left. At the highest point, and beyond the easy passage afforded by the bank, turn right to avoid cliffs ahead. Descend sharply to a stream which plunges alarmingly into Swiss Valley below: hopefully not too alarmingly because you have to follow it.

To do this, walk to a ruin on the opposite bank, looking out here for a grassy and therefore well-hidden path zig-zagging down into the valley far below. This path may be both a little difficult to find and when found quite easy to lose. One hint: initially it slants for a comparatively long distance away from the right bank of the stream.

On the floor of Swiss Valley and still on the path, turn left to follow a fence on the right and then cross a gate. With cliffs on the left and forest on the right, keep on a track close to the latter and follow it into forest on both sides. Turn right at the major forest track (it's the Old Bog Road again). Ignoring a left turn shortly after, walk down the track through forest to the main road. Turn left and walk the short distance to the carpark.

Notes

1. Fr.O'Rorke, whom we meet more than once in this book as a late 19th century writer on the history and geography of the Sligo area, was much taken with Glencar Waterfall: *"(it)...affords as much gratification to the eye as to the ear. At any time through the year (it is a) striking sight as its body of water leaps from ledge to ledge, down precipices of some hundred feet high"*.

2. There are two crannógs in Glencar Lough, one at each end, and the eastern one should be visible on the ascent. These little wooded islands are lake dwellings of the Early Christian period, though they continued in use up to the 17th century. The word *'crann'* appropriately means tree and the basic material of most crannógs is wood, whether for piling or for the dwelling (there was usually only one) that was built on the timber foundation. Their inconvenient siting obviously suggests an easily defended location.

One of these crannógs is said, according to the records of the Four Masters, to have been the scene of a tragic event in the year 1029, when more than sixty local noblemen were burned to death. The crannóg must have been much bigger then than it is now.

Walk 16　　　Hangman's Hill

A grisly off-putting name for a most inviting mountain. Hangman's Hill lies as close the centre of the Castlegal Range as any other peak and gives a superb grandstand view of most of the range. Though grassy and somewhat bland from nearby Glencar, its top is far from bland with undulating peaklets and sudden declivities dipping dramatically into bogland to its west. The delights of the heights are prefaced by an easy and lovely ascent and followed by a steep and equally lovely descent. A most attractive walk.

Walking time: Distance 5.5km/3.5miles, climb 340m/1100 ft, walking time 2hrs 15 mins, thus allowing some extra time for a steep descent.

Largy, Glenade

Transport: Start at the same point as route 8. The table 282 bus service might also be used.

Map: 1:50000 sheet 16.

Terrain and Navigational Difficulties: Track and path at the start, followed by some rough ground to the top. Some wet and steep ground towards the finish where care is necessary. The narrow distinctive north-west nose of Hangman's Hill and the forest near the top reduce already modest navigational difficulties.

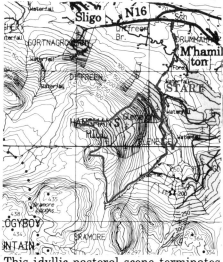

Route: Take the right fork at the start and ascend steeply, passing the return track on the right a little way up. Less than 1km/half-mile further on, where an occupied house is nestled low into the hillside, fork right (south-west) to follow a grassy track into hilly country.

Take this track steadily upwards, noting on the left old field boundaries ineffectively breaking up rough grassy grazing land and further up a delightful stream descending precipitously via occasional low waterfalls.

This idyllic pastoral scene terminates at a gate at which two streams meet. Follow the right tributary upstream keeping it on the left, and immediately Hangman's Hill looms ahead, or rather two of its tops, the right one of which you should now climb.

After this first top head west across a tiny valley to the highest top keeping forest some way off on the right (this forest is shown on the OS map reaching somewhat higher up than in reality). Curiously no spot height is given for this highest point but it just tops the 400m (1312ft) mark, an academic point and probably of little interest compared to the marvellous view unfolded before you.

From here head to the prominent nose to the north-west and reached, not by a direct route - this would take you over cliffs - but by a swing roughly north and then west. To reach its tip cross a fence which will prove useful on the descent.

Having assimilated the views from here return to the fence, cross it again and immediately veer gradually away from it to pick an old field boundary crossing the hillside just north of the nose. Take it across the hill to near the top corner of the plantation and descend directly, forest on the right to a ruin below which a stream cascades over limestone slabs. A little further down, at about the hawthorn bushes, look out for a convenient place on the right at which to cross the stream and reach the end of a forest track. Clear-felling is currently (spring 1992) taking place here but the forest track will stay in spite of other changes in the area. Take the track to its end and turn left here for the start.

Walk 17   The Doons

The small steep-sided flat-topped limestone hills of the Doons are unique in Ireland and form a highly scenic area for pottering and wandering without a detailed plan. For this reason the route described here is a modest suggestion to get you into the heart of the area: once there you will probably have your own ideas of where to walk.

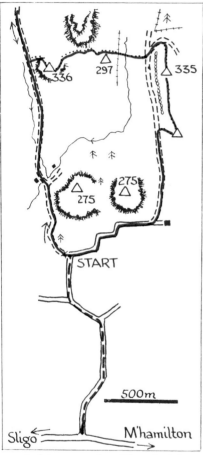

Walking time: Distance 4.5km/2.5 miles, climb 270m/900ft, walking time 1 hr 45 mins (in theory). However this is an area whose complicated terrain demands, and whose diversity invites, slow progress so leave about 2hrs 30mins to walk at a leisurely pace.

Transport: Access is from the unnumbered but good road parallel to and north of the R286. Two ways of getting to the start are given here but whichever direction you are approaching from, note the handball alley mentioned below as it is a good landmark.

From Parke's Castle drive east (so that the Castle is passed on the right), turn first left, drive to the top of the road, turn left and watch out here for the handball alley on the right. Turn first right 0.3 miles farther on, and swing right so keeping to the 'main' road after another 0.5 miles. Park at the sandpit after 0.2 miles (GR 785374).

To get there directly from Manorhamilton, take the N16 towards Sligo, turn left onto the R286, and keep straight on rather than taking the turn left signposted Dromahair. The handball alley is on the right past Leckaun post office.The table 277 or 281 buses might also be used.

Map: 1:50000 sheet 16 or 25 though they fail to do full justice to a complex and varied topography. The sketch map given here is a limited though maybe acceptable alternative.

Terrain and Navigational Difficulties: one extremely mucky farmyard to be squelched through at the start (it can be avoided by facing instead other hazards eg wet fields and fences): otherwise intermittent path and varied pathless ground. With lots of prominent landmarks few navigational problems.

Route: Cross the gate left of the sandpit and take the track beyond it, forest on the right, to a farm just before which the track divides. Here you must decide whether to keep left to brave the farmyard with its mud (or possibly worse) or to detour right and cross up through fields and so emerge comparatively unscathed onto the left track some distance up beyond the farmyard.

At this point, on the track beyond (north of) the farm, you might like to consider the landmarks around. To the south lies Doon 275m whose western flank you have just rounded (we shall refer to all small flat-topped hills around here as 'Doons') and which has forest draped elegantly round its shoulders, but not completely covering it as shown on the 1:50000 map. To its left is its unforested sister Doon (also about 275m). Looking ahead north is Doon 336m and as we advance the great rocky prow of Sramore rears to the right and the Keelogyboy massif to the left.

It is well worth while wandering up this track to the broad pass between Kellogyboy and Sramore to catch a glimpse of the shoulder of Hangman's Hill directly ahead. However let's turn back at this pass thus facing Doon 336m again. It now appears to the left of the track as a lopsided plateau, lower on the right. Close to the Doon cross the fence to your left to climb limestone ramparts to its top, a top surrounded by a curious grassy wall and offering a lofty eyrie from which to view the surrounding country far and wide.

The next task is to contour round the nearby rocky nose of Sramore which lies directly to the east. To do this keep to the intermittent more or less level path as far as the huge boulders blocking, or at least impeding, the way ahead. A short detour among these rocks is worth the effort (and risk of a twisted ankle) especially if you are interested in the fossils that embellish them.

However the direct route is down between Sramore's nose and a flattish grassy protuberance (not a Doon) at its foot, marked on the map as 297m. Keep this on the right to cross a fence (carefully!) and a narrow stream and so reach higher and drier land at a track. Turn left here and take the nearby fork right so heading to the corner of a forestry plantation peeping over the hillside ahead.

Near this corner, and you are now on the western side of the Fawnlion massif, turn right (south) and for the best views stay on its edge keeping a stone wall a little way off on the right. Continue along this massif edge to point 335m and climb the last Doon, a short but distinct rise to about 295m. Turn right steeply downhill here to reach the track, turn left and take it down to a farmhouse at a 'major' road (it's amazing how what one thought of as a pot-holed road improves to one of good quality after a short time on tracks). Follow it round three right angle bends under the partly forested cliffs of the Doons 275m to the start.

Notes
R.L.Praeger, the distinguished Irish naturalist, says of the Doons: *"The ground immediately adjoining the north side of Lough Gill is full of surprises: there are little cliff-walled flat-topped limestone hills with unexpected lakelets among them and deep ferny glens: the queer bare limestone mountains rise on one side and the tree-embosomed lake stretches on the other"*.

How did these strange hills scattered over the southern side of the Castlegal Range originate? It appears that they were originally formed as reefs in an ancient sea. Reefs, consisting of mounds of the shelly remains of corals and other fossils, are at present developing in many places in the world, notably in the South Pacific. In the case of the Doons the sea receded and they were left embedded in strata of softer limestone that was deposited alongside the reefs. When this was eroded by weathering the harder rock of the reefs was left protruding above the general level.

Walk 18   Sandy Lough

The short walk to Sandy Lough gives good views back over the valley of Rossinver and towards the hills of Saddle and Dough. From the lough the walk can be extended to form a rough rectangle. This involves crossing bogland, walking down a lovely track beside a stream banked by tiny woods and finishing on country roads, partly in remote hilly country, back to the start.

Walking Time: For the short walk distance 3km/2miles, climb 140m/460ft, walking time 1 hr. For the long walk distance 10km/6.5miles, climb 310m/1000ft, walking time 3 hrs 15 mins. (A kind non-walking driver might pick the walkers up on the R282 to avoid a tedious tramp of over a mile uphill at the end.)

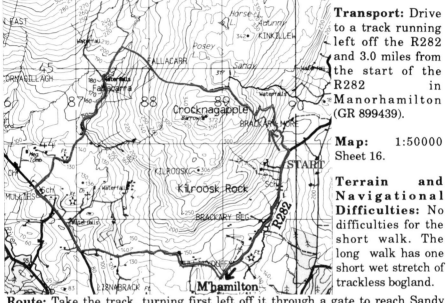

Transport: Drive to a track running left off the R282 and 3.0 miles from the start of the R282 in Manorhamilton (GR 899439).

Map: 1:50000 Sheet 16.

Terrain and Navigational Difficulties: No difficulties for the short walk. The long walk has one short wet stretch of trackless bogland.

Route: Take the track, turning first left off it through a gate to reach Sandy Lough, a rather large body of water which does not offer much shelter or seclusion. For the *short* walk return directly or after inspecting three other smaller lakes in the immediate vicinity.

For the *long* walk take the left fork near the lake, continue to the track's end and hence straight on over bogland at present (spring 1992) chewed up by machinery. The gradual descent reveals a rectangle of light-coloured vegetation. This is new forestry and you should keep it on the left as you approach it, thus crossing a stream. Turn left onto the track beyond the stream and walk down by it, a lovely stretch of cascades and bank-side trees. At the tee turn left and left again onto the 'main' road (it runs parallel to the R280 in Glenade). Where this road swings right continue straight ahead for a further 700m and take the turn left that is just after a bridge and at the top of a short but sharp rise.

From here it's a straight-forward walk on tarmac (and pothole) to the R282 across the southern upland of the Dartry Hills, through marginal, remote hilly farmland. At the R282 turn left for the start if no car is awaiting you.

The Bricklieve Mountains (signposting tends to favour the term 'Carrowkeel') are an area of steep-sided mountain blocks close to the N4 (Sligo-Dublin road) about 26km/16miles south of Sligo. Their chief attraction are the numerous passage grave cemeteries sited on the hillsides, but the low, cliff-bound plateaus, separated by long grassy trenches, are a bonus for the hill walker. An area that merits that overworked adjective 'unique'.

Walking Time: The author took 3 hrs 15 mins walking (and stumbling and blundering) time which suggests that the standard time of about 2 hours based on a modest distance of 6.5km/4miles and climb of 240m/800ft is grossly inadequate. This is an area of high vegetation and short but not easily negotiable cliffs which greatly slow progress. You might also wish to allow time to potter around the six passage graves visited.

Transport: By car take the N4 to the village of Castlebaldwin. Turn right here (if coming from Sligo) and follow the signs to the passage graves for 2.0 miles (not indefinitely), watching out just before this distance for a farm on the left just beyond which you should turn left. Park at the turn right a few hundred metres farther on (G R 743122). (You can take this right turn and drive along it for a short distance but it is difficult to park on it and is barred by gates so it is hardly worth it.)

The table 275 bus service might be used to get to Castlebaldwin.

Map: 1:50000 sheet 25. The sketch map shown here gives a few more details of the complicated terrain than the OS map. Lake Availe, which is marked on the OS map, no longer exists.

Terrain and Navigational Difficulties: Mostly trackless and as stated above not the easiest of terrain.Give yourself lots of time!

Route: This is pre-eminently a pottering area and the route given is only a suggestion in an area where you are unlikely to get lost and where your car is never going to be far away (in distance that is, time is another matter).

Take the turn right (south). As shown on the sketch map the nearest grave is on the hill to the right above cliffs but bad vegetation makes it tedious to access and these cliffs mean an equally tedious retracing of steps, so let's omit it. Instead turn first left and left again to cross a bridge and when close to high ground on the right leave the track to climb to two graves [1], the more northerly of which is the only oval one of the group.

From this grave, walk east and then south to keep to the high ground and then cross a narrow trench at a wall which spans the trench's breadth. Ascend the northern end of the hill on the other side of the trench, where there are four graves and a large swampy hollow (10 metres of so across) which might act as a reassuring landmark.

The next block of mountain is the most difficult to gain and the route to it the most interesting. First walk to the eastern side of the block of mountain you are on. Then turn south along a grassy level stretch bounded by rocks and an intermittent tiny cliff on the right and by a low but not negotiable cliff on the left. Below the latter is a narrow grassy trench, spanned by a stone wall which half-heartedly climbs part way up the slope opposite.

Continue until you are close to the wall and, where impassable bushes block the way ahead, descend left through them, a difficult but not dangerous passage. Once in open ground descend over another tiny cliff and climb the opposite side of the trench, keeping the stone wall on the right.

Climb to the upper end of the wall and then veer right over steep grassy ground to avoid another line of cliffs. Having circumnavigated these, at level ground above turn left over fern-covered ground to another two graves, on the way admiring

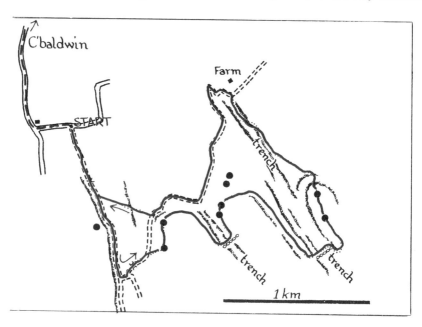

nearby Lough Arrow. From the more northerly grave descend carefully over yet another two sets of short cliffs on the northern edge of the block. This edge overlooks a limestone pavement and stone circles.

Walk west from the pavement to yet, another line of cliffs beyond which is the same trench crossed earlier, here narrower and even more grassy. Keep close above the cliffs on the left for a while, descending where possible into the trench.

Turn north along the trench and left onto a crossways track rising steeply corkscrew-like over the northern end of the second block crossed earlier. Continue along it around the first block from where you will see the initial track of the day and your beckoning car. A direct route back looks to be a tempting short-cut over seemingly easy ground. It *is* a short cut but the ground is not all that easy and of course there is another short cliff to descend, so it is only just about worth taking. Once on the track turn right for the start.

Notes

The Bricklieve Mountains constitute a splendid example of karstic limestone country. They contain swallow holes (where water has sunk directly through the permeable limestone leaving a depression a metre or so across, a geological phenomenon described in more detail under route 29), dry valleys (valleys which have never held rivers or whose rivers have disappeared underground), caves and limestone pavements.

1. It seems that these passage graves were built before the bog invaded the area. At that time the hills would have been littered with limestone blocks thus making the construction job a lot easier.

R.L.Praeger, the naturalist, was the first person to enter one of the burial chambers which lie beneath the piles of stone. He gives a vivid account of this memorable occasion in 'The Way that I Went':

"I (was) the first to crawl down the entrance-passage, and I did so with no little awe. I lit three candles and stood awhile, to let my eyes accustom themselves to the dim light. There was everything just as the last Bronze Age man had left it, three or four thousand years before. A light brownish dust covered all. The central chamber was empty, but each of the three recesses opening from it contained much burnt bone debris, with flat stones on which evidently the bones had been carried in, after the bodies had been cremated in strong fires outside".

He goes on to describe implements made from the bones of bear, wild boar and oxen found in the chamber.

As a contrast how about this technically uncompromising start to an article about the configuration of the passage graves which eventually leads to God-know-what cosmic conclusion. It is entitled 'Earth Energies and Etheric Energies' and was written in 1986.

"We have discussed how the Earth Stars cover our surface in spherical three dimensional form to build up our aura and how the standard star is the basic atom of the macrocosm-stretching out in expanding spirals - interlocking and interpermeating through space...."

Follow that if you can!

Benwiskin

43

Walk 20   Slieve Deane

"the yellow pool has overflowed high up on Clooth-na-Bare,
For the wet winds are blowing out of the clinging air"
(Red Hanrahan's Song about Ireland).

A fairly short walk but if you do the full route, not an easy one. The stroll to Lough Lumman is a steady uphill along sylvan tracks and open moorland but a different proposition awaits beyond the lake. From there, the climb to 'nearby' peaks is over high vegetation and innocent-looking terrain which conceals deep steep-sided channels. A stroll or a challenge - your choice.

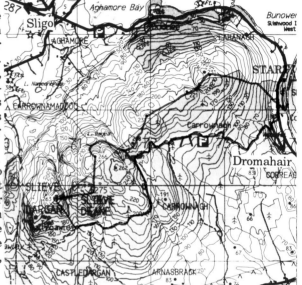

Walking Time: Distance 5.5km/3miles, climb 160m /500ft, walking time 1hr 45mins for the short walk. Distance 9.5km/6miles, climb 500m/1650ft, walking time roughly 5 hrs (allowing 1hr 15mins extra for rough terrain) for the long.

Transport: From Sligo take the N4 turning left towards Dromahair after about two miles. Park in the forest carpark on the left (at GR 739314), the second one along this road, after a further 3.5 miles.

Map: 1:50000 sheet 25. The actual area under forest is not nearly as extensive as that depicted on this map and in particular does not extend onto the higher ground of the range.

Terrain and Navigational Difficulties: The short route has tracks for most of the way, but most of the long route is trackless with some very rough terrain. The one serious navigational difficulty is indicated in the text below but otherwise only average care is required.

Route: From the carpark turn left and walk for about five minutes passing on the way a curious forked concrete driveway right. Turn next right onto a track leading into a delightful wooded area and farther up, where it has narrowed to a path, through some less delightful gorse bushes.

An elegant if incongruously located garden gate marks the point of release from gorse. Beyond it continue up painlessly through a forest plantation initially on both sides, and later only on the right. At the top of this plantation turn left to follow a fence and at a fence tee farther up where a narrow tongue of forest creeps up on the left, gird your loins for navigational difficulties.

The aim is to take the bridleway across the bogland to a wide track not more than 30 minutes walk away. This bridleway is marked by occasional horse's hoof prints and yellow paint splashes but they are not easy to follow in the rough terrain, so a compass bearing of 240 degrees might be prudent. You might also note that you should veer away from the forest on the left.

At the above-mentioned wide track turn right and walk to Lough Lumman, a good spot for a repast and contemplation of the immediate future, namely whether to press on. If you decide to do so, continue onwards on the track to a straight section hemmed in by high bushes, swing right beyond them and after another five minutes where the track swings uncompromisingly left continue straight ahead on a muddy path. Forest comes in close on the left and after some clumps of particularly spiky gorse on the right, strike off right to the nearest hill avoiding rough ground as best you can on the ascent. This is the first of four neighbouring hills, three of which are on the route and all four of which are guarded by trenches, 50m/160ft or so deep and walled by steep slopes of high vegetation, useful (and indeed in places necessary) as makeshift substitute ropes on the ascents[1].

Slieve Dargan (263m/853ft), the first hill to be climbed has a ring of stones on the summit. It commands good views west towards Knocknarea and Ballysadare Bay. Slieve Deane (275m/905ft) the next summit, is directly to the east and is crowned by a trig pillar. The climb to it is greatly supplemented by the rise from the first trench, which is initially hidden. Continue north down into another trench and thence up to Slieve Dagea (266m/872ft), which has two cairns. (You will note that the tops though close and otherwise similar have distinguishing marks.) Drop to Lough Dagea and contour round point 262m, the hill to the south-east, to meet the corner of an earth bank whose dark green vegetation makes it quite distinctive. Follow it north-eastwards, Lough Lumman below on the right, along the top of the ridge running towards Lough Gill.

Close to the unnamed hill, point 231m/761ft and still following the earth bank, drop into a last trench, mercifully a shallow one, and then climb this hill, which gives excellent views of Lough Gill. Here the earth bank swings right and loses itself in broken country, so you must descend east without the guiding bank. This descent to the road is through high vegetation and low but wicked slabs: the occasional traces of paths seem designed to dash tentatively awakening hopes by abruptly heading in the wrong direction. Near the road veer right to the edge of a forestry plantation and cross into it to meet a forest track. Walk the few metres to the forest entrance, turn left onto the road and right for the carpark.

Notes.
Slieve Deane features, as Birds Mountain, in a story of W.B. Yeats: *"Such a mortal too was Clooth-na-Bare, who went all over the world seeking a lake deep enough to drown the faery life of which she had grown weary, leaping from hill to lake to hill and setting up a cairn of stones where ever her feet lighted, until and last she found the deepest water in the world in little Lough Ia [Lough Dagea], on top of the Birds Mountain at Sligo"*.

1. These ravines, locally known as 'alts', are a feature of the Ox Mountains, of which the Slieve Daene area forms a part, geologically if not geographically. They generally run north-south though in this area they are nearer north-west to south-east.

Walk 21   Leean

This area, steep hummocks of short grassy sward, is as easy as a carpet to walk on and, for comparatively little effort offers wide and delightful views of rugged terrain. Strangely, it is the muddy tracks at the end of the walk that are the most difficult to walk so that if you wish to avoid these, a direct return from the top of Leean is recommended.

Walking Time: Distance 7.5km/4.5miles, climb 340m /1100ft, walking time 2 hrs 30 mins.

Transport: Turn south (ie left from Manorhamilton) off the N16 onto the R286, drive 1.4 miles and turn right up a rough road to a tee. Park around here at GR 833389.

Map: 1:50000 sheet 16,25 or 26, the first of these better for identifying landmarks.

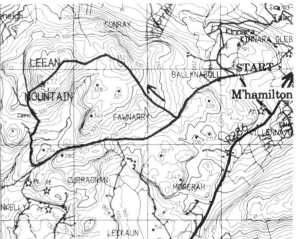

Terrain and Navigational Difficulties: The terrain is noted above. The outlying hummocks of Leean might cause navigational uncertainty but the main summit towers above the others and moreover it has a prominent trig pillar visible from afar.

Route: From the tee walk west along the track, forest on the right. Where the track levels out just before the first farm turn right off it and climb directly to point 352m[1]. Drop slightly into an upland valley, noting here, purely for reassurance, a small sheep fold and continue on to the main peak of Leean (417m/1368ft, perhaps *Liagán*, a pillar stone), crowned by the above-mentioned trig pillar, and so making the name in Irish particularly appropriate.

From Leean descend steeply south or less steeply south-west to a track and follow it down between outliers of Leean to a tee. Turn left here to a lonely deserted building and continue onwards on the track which here requires an act of faith to believe in, so nebulous has it become. Where it does resume it is extremely muddy so that you may ruefully conclude that its former nebulous condition was far preferable. Continue straight onwards to the start.

Longer Variation: See under Walk 22 for a longer walk combining these two routes.

Note.

1 Somewhere on this side of Leean is an unusual geological balancing act: a limestone pedestal supporting an erratic boulder. This boulder of hard durable rock came to rest here after being carried by a glacier. The bedrock limestone has long ago been eroded away except where it is protected by the more durable boulder above it and the result is a 'mushroom', the large boulder supported on a comparatively slender column of limestone. Unfortunately the author has not come upon this interesting phenomenon: apart from being 'east of Leean' the only other information given to locate it is that it lies at a height of 347m/1137ft.

Walk 22   Benbo

The initial section through an old wood of hazel and holly ends at a viewpoint overlooking Manorhamilton. A stiff climb ensues to the tops of Benbo, which command fine views especially towards the nearby Castlegal Range. The walk ends with a steep heathery descent and a country road.

Walking Time: Distance 6.5km/4miles, climb 340m/1100ft, walking time 2 hrs 15 mins.

Transport: From the main crossroads in Manorhamilton drive 1.0 miles towards Sligo along the N16, turn left here and right after another 1.3 miles. Drive for another 0.3 miles and park on the road-side at GR 861367 near a partly concealed grassy track heading directly away from the right of the road.

Map: 1:50000 sheet 16,25 or 26.

Terrain and Navigational Difficulties: The ground is generally wet, particularly so on the final climb to the top: there are no navigational difficulties.

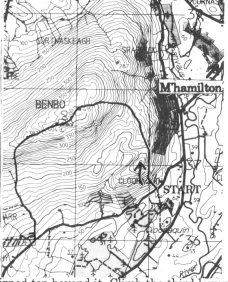

Route: Take the track (further up it relegates itself to a path) through the old wood and zig-zag upwards past a forestry plantation[1] on the right, forking left at level ground near its end (the viewpoint to Manorhamilton is on the right fork). Climb from here to the cairn on the top of Benbo (415m/1365ft, perhaps *Beann Bo*, peak of cows) by following a grassy ramp, walk to Black Lough and ascend the second cairned top beyond it. Climb the third lower uncairned top and then continue a little along the left of the spur running south-west, watching out here for a straight path traversing the bogland below.

Descend steeply to this path and walk downhill to its end at a fence. Turn right here to cross a stile and at the ruin beyond take the driveway to tarmac. Turn left here for the start about 1.5km/1 mile away.

Longer Variation: This walk may easily be combined with Walk 21. Take Walk 22 to the third summit of Benbo, drop north-west off the summit ridge to reach the R286 between two stretches of plantation and take Walk 21 from there.

Note.

1. As you climb beyond the forestry plantation you will see how bog vegetation has filled what would otherwise be a sharp rocky defile down on the left. Bogs are an invaluable 'source book' of the vegetational history of the surrounding area. Pollen from plants growing around the bog are blown onto its surface and are eventually buried and preserved in its anaerobic (oxygenless) depths. A hollow tube can be inserted vertically down into the bog and the pollen of the resulting core sample analysed. With the aid of carbon-dating a profile of the rise and decay of plants and trees over the millennia can be charted.

Walk 23   Glenfarne Plateau East

Glenfarne Plateau is shaped like a very fat U whose base faces north-west abutting the O'Donnell's Rock area. Its highest points (hardly justifying the epithet 'peaks') attain 400m/1300ft over large areas though the plateau nowhere reaches 450m/1500ft. Not very inspiring? Well, certainly not in bad weather but in good with long views and the best of the terrain underfoot lovely walks may be had with little effort.

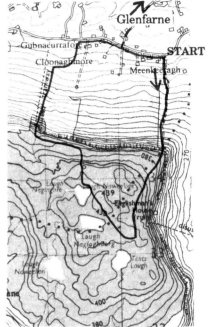

This first route in the area wanders around the northern arm of the U. 'Wanders around' is an appropriate term because the large lakes of the plateau, scattered randomly like fruit in a cherry cake, make a logical route impossible to devise: that described here is but one illogical route among many.

Walking Time: Distance 8km/5miles, climb 330m/1100ft, walking time 3 hrs, allowing some time to cross high heather.

Transport: Drive to Glenfarne on the N16. Note that the Glenfarne of the signposts at the village is not the Glenfarne of the 1:50000 map. The upshot is that, travelling east, you should turn right just after the turn left for Kiltyclogher (R281). Drive to the top of the road, turn left here and drive for 0.4 miles to a gated track right just before a stream (at GR 006356). (Please try to ignore the untidy appearance of this area.)

The table 282 bus service might also be used to get to the start.

Map: 1:50000 sheet 26.

Terrain and Navigational Difficulties: On the plateau the terrain is surprisingly firm, with areas of short heather and boulders. The navigational problems are minor: the cliffs are not nearly as alarming as they appear to be on the map, being impassable only along short stretches of the east-facing edge and the lakes are prominent, almost unmissable landmarks on the plateau.

Route: Take the gated track steadily upwards, passing a forestry plantation on the right and at its top ascend through boulders to the plateau. Continue southwards, watching out below left for the unimpressive ruins of the "Englishman's House"[1] and more immediately for long rifts in the ground underfoot. Ascend the high ground south of the ruins so coming within a few hundred metres of Tents Lough (*teinte*, fires). From here the route continues

Glenaniff

north-west to Loughs Nagloghderg (*Loch na gCloch Dearg*, lake of the red stones) and Naweeloge. However, if you want to wander around even more aimlessly than this route does you might like to note that a ridge of slightly higher firmer ground runs north-east from Lough Naweelion (*Loch na bhFaoilean*, lake of the seagulls) with a linear swamp on its south-east side and that there is a prominent cairn to the north-east of Tents Lough and close to it. The most important landmark however is the trig pillar 250m north of Lough Naweeloge and it is here that the route resumes with renewed definiteness.

Descend north-west from the trig pillar to the minor drop facing north. Walk west along here through high heather and at a gap between two forestry plantations descend northwards by a lovely waterfall into wet swampy ground. Continue down to a minor track leading to a wider forestry track (neither shown on the map), turn right onto this wider track and take it to the tarmac. Turn right here for the start.

Notes.
1. The memoirs of the Geological Survey, published in 1886, seem to refer indirectly to the "Englishman's House" and the tramways both here and more impressively on the north side of the plateau, all of which are discernible on the ground (just about). The memoirs state: *"East of Tents Lough there are some very slight indications of coal, utterly worthless: but there are some of the oldest inhabitants who remember some English miners having lived in a hut on the hillside for the purpose of working the coal'.*

Walk 24   Glenfarne Plateau West

The comments given under route 23 apply equally well to this part of the Glenfarne Plateau, with two modifications. Firstly, that the higher ground is protected by a bulwark of low cliffs or by ramparts of sandstone boulders above which the ground is quite firm. Secondly that the landmarks lend themselves to a slightly more elegant route.

Walking Time: Distance 12km/7.5miles,climb 340m/1100ft, walking time 3hrs 45mins.

Transport: Drive to Tawnylea (GR 899284) off the R280, from which the tiny village is signposted. Now careful! If you were standing at the post office and with your back to it you would have to turn right and take the first right to get onto the correct road. In short, head north-east. Drive for 1.2 miles to a laneway on the left at abandoned buildings (GR 913295).

Map: 1:50000 sheet 26.

Terrain and Navigational Difficulties: The terrain is wetter on the slog up to and down from the plateau than it is on it. Navigation is also a little tricky in the same area. Note that the map does not show the full extent of the forestry plantations climbing up the south-west side of the plateau nor all the forest tracks, and this omission demands additional concentration.

Route: Walk uphill on the minor road, cross a gate and enter forest at another gate. Continue straight up at a crossroads and at open ground beyond head directly for Lough Altscrahagh, whose northern side reveals a wedge of new forestry. Since you are likely to be returning this way a close study of the terrain from the forest to the lake might be no bad idea.

Follow the inlet stream uphill keeping it on your left as this bank is slightly drier. Near its source you may be lucky enough to find a tumbled sheep fold, an indication that you are on course (it does not mean that you are not on course if you don't find it). Continue north to climb the sandstone boulders marking the edge of higher ground so reaching a trig pillar (about GR 932322) not marked on the map.

The next stretch is north-west along high and firm ground. Lough Strand (*Straithean*, a flat place) initially on the right. Among the many hills and other mountain features to be seen the great dip of Glenade and the tumbled mass of the Castlegal Range in the middle distance are the most dramatic.

Idle contemplation of the scenery directly ahead is brought to an abrupt end at the low cliffs marking the north-west rim of the plateau. Here you must turn south-west to Lackagh Lough, thus following irregular cliffs which lead into rough and treacherous ground concealing deep holes near the lake. Just to its north are the Two Sisters. It is unusual on Irish OS maps to name rocks, but these are unusual rocks: really mighty compared to the many others around and looking to the untutored eye (eg the author's) as if they formerly constituted one really massive boulder that has been cleft in twain.

From Lackagh Lough a compass bearing is advisable to find the next lake to the south, Lough Carran. If the weather is clear, approach from its western side where a band of high bumpy ground whose crest offers good views extends from its western corner. This is an attractive lake, nestling among boulders in steep rock-strewn ground rather than lying squarely and exposed on moorland as others in this area.

At Lough Carran a decision: you can opt for an adventurous finish by walking along the outlet stream down to forest and then following the variation given below or you can choose the easier finish which will now be described.

A forest fence runs east from Lough Carran and you should follow it to its corner just north-east of Lough Altscrahagh and from here head directly to the end of the track on which you started. If on this stretch you cross a fence at a part of an iron bedstead acting as an improvised gate then veer right to find the track. Take this track directly back to the start.

A Short, Long Variation: This is short in distance, long in time - and demanding in effort. The forest break starting at GR 918307 and running south-west for 800m/half-mile offers one way of negotiating the plantation. But be warned! It is bounded on one side by a precipitous slope ending at a stream and on the other by massed forest only penetrable at the very end of the stretch. The margin between these two sets of hazards is in places disconcertingly narrow. One morsel of consolation: you can follow either bank as there is a bridge at the bottom (but note axiom: the other bank *always* looks easier). Once out of forest turn left, swing left uphill with the track where a minor track runs temptingly downhill right and turn right at the crossroads for the start.

Note
You will have passed the ironworks on the left on the way to the starting point. From 1852 or so to 1858 ironstone was mined on the south-west slopes of the Glenfarne Plateau, an area which you will traverse on the ascent. The ironworks consisted of two large blast furnaces, a steam-engine and engine house and ancillary buildings. Unfortunately the enterprise went bankrupt in 1859 as did another company on the same site shortly after. This latter company used local turf for smelting, surely an early example of the industrial use of the ubiquitous native fuel.

A cannon constructed here saw service in the Crimean War, but this was probably a dubious consolation to the workers who were shortly afterwards to be thrown out of work. Dubliners may be interested to note that the Ha'penny Bridge in the centre of the city is constructed from iron made in these works, as a plaque on the side of the bridge declares.

Walk 25   Glencar: The Northern Cliffs

*"— — — There is a waterfall
Upon Ben Bulben side
That all my childhood counted dear"*   (Towards Break of Day)

A spectacular walk along the cliffs and steep ground on the edge of the
Benbulbin Plateau. The views are excellent: a variety of cliff and tree-clothed
slope, Glencar Lough itself and the curious grassy hummocks wedged between
cliffs and the valley floor. With a good deal of hill and valley terrain to be
negotiated along an intermittent cliff edge this is a more demanding walk than
initially appears.

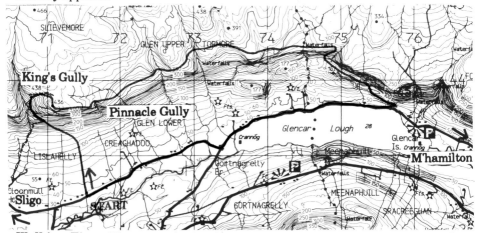

Walking Time: Distance 13km/8miles, climb 600m/2000ft, walking time 4 hrs
30 mins using one car. This may be reduced to 3 hrs 30 mins if a second car is
left at Glencar Lough as described below.

Transport: Car to GR 715424 on the minor road that runs along the southern
side of the Benbulbin Plateau. To get there take the N15 from Sligo, turn right at
Rathcormack church, turn right at the tee just over a mile further on and drive
another 1.4 miles to a prominent guest house on the left. Park considerately.

If coming from the Glencar or Manorhamilton direction drive along the northern
shore of the lake, turn right immediately after it and drive for another 1.3 miles
to the guest house. A second car might be left at GR 760434, a carpark on the
lakeside at the eastern end of Glencar Lough, 2.9 miles from the start. To get
there from the start drive away from Sligo turning left at the tee.

The table 282 bus might also be used.

Map: 1:50000 sheet 16.

Terrain and Navigational Difficulties: Pathless except for two short
stretches of track and of course the road walk at the end. Cliff edges are usually
easy to follow but this one is intermittent,so beware of deceptively easily sloped
ground which could steepen lower down into dangerous cliffs.

Route: The initial target is King's Gully, seen from the start far to the left along the
cliffs rearing majestically two-layered to the north. Take the track immediately to

the left of the guest house and continue past a ruin through rushy fields. Near open land at the foot of the scree slopes cross the boulder wall on the left running uphill and, climbing diagonally left, watch out for the grassy track leading into King's Gully. It doesn't matter if you don't find it at first: you will eventually.

Follow the track into King's Gully, a defile which gradually narrows and deepens into an impressive canyon. Where its extension as a path definitely levels off , turn right off it to pass a small war memorial[1] (reassuring if found but not essential) on the way to the bumpy tops to the east.

From the tops continue along low cliffs to Pinnacle Gully, a prominent and dramatic detached segment. As noted above these cliffs offer an easy passage to the grassy slopes below but be warned that beyond these are the main vertical cliffs, so that there is no escape route here.

Beyond Pinnacle Gully pass a ruin in a shallow valley and from here climb along a wall which runs along the southern side of the hill ahead. Beyond the hill drop into a very narrow valley spanned by a disused dam and climb again to pass under a power line and bucket cable system, both formerly used in the mines farther north[2]. Past these watch out for curious rifts in the limestone, deep channels rather ineffectively fenced to deter sheep. Beyond these cross another stream which falls over shallow limestone pavements. Its claim to fame is unfortunately not visible from here [3].

Farther on cross a third stream, one which plunges down a grassy slope to Swiss Valley, a tiny fern-floored glen tucked in between the cliffs of the plateau's rim on one side and a small wooded ridge on the other[4]. Do not descend here, instead climb the hillside beyond the stream through high heather, keeping close to the cliff to avail of an earth bank which offers considerably easier going.

The bank eventually bends left to run parallel to a forestry plantation. Cross the fence close to the start of this plantation and turn right downhill at the forest track visible just beyond. This takes you directly down to the road that runs along the northern side of Glencar (*Gleann na Chairtha,* the glen of the standing stone). If you have no transport here, it is a long (5km/3miles) but pleasant walk to the start particularly in the initial stages along the lake. Don't forget to turn right at its end.

Notes.
1. Here six members of the anti-treaty forces were killed in the civil war in 1922. Five were locals from County Sligo, the sixth the son of the co-founder of the Gaelic League.
2. Mining in this area is more fully discussed under Walk 33.
3. This is *Sruth-in-aghaidh-an-Aird* ('the stream against the height'). A 19th century historian says: 'When the wind blows strongly from the west, the spectacle is nothing short of sublime, as the rushing rivulet, having reached the edge of the precipice, instead of rolling down, in accordance with the laws of gravitation, gets caught, as it were, in some great chemical laboratory, which resolves it into its original elements...'
   In truth this is a by no means uncommon phenomenon when a strong wind is deflected upwards by the face of a cliff. The upward wind counteracts gravity and blows the waterfall up as a plume of spray. There is a better-known example at Kinder Scout in the Peak District. Yeats briefly and vividly described it: *"The cataract smokes upon the mountain side".*
4. The origin of these strange ridges and their enclosed valleys (two others are visible to the west) is outlined under walk 28.

Walk 26   Thur

Thur mountain, whose southern side rises gently above Glenfarne (it is too modest to dominate) is the most easterly of the block of mountainside running eastward from Rossinver. However, the most memorable topographical feature surrounding Thur is not mountain but the interplay of land and water: the two Lough Macneans near at hand and the large expanse of Lough Melvin among others, farther off. To gain these excellent views of lake and wooded islands a little purgatorial bogland must be endured at the start and even more at the end. There is also a road walk, a long but pleasant one, which can be broken by a visit to the national monument of Sean McDermott's house.

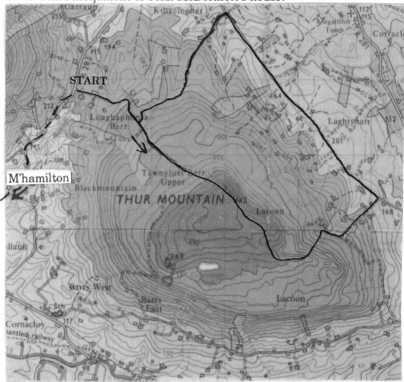

Walking time: Distance 12km/7.5miles, climb 400m/1300 ft, walking time 4 hrs 30 mins (allowing 30 mins extra for bad terrain) for the whole walk, but this can be reduced to 6km/3.5miles, climb 240m/800ft, walking time 2 hrs if a car is available on the side road at GR 001404 near Sean McDermott's house.

Transport: From Manorhamilton take the N16 east, branch left onto the R283 (Kiltyclogher road) and drive a further 3.6 miles to park at the side road on the right at GR 959418. (Watch out for the unexpected left turn on the R283 after 1.6 miles on it.)

The Saturday only table 282 bus service might also be used.

Map: 1:50000 sheet 17 with a tiny section on sheet 26. Unfortunately this section is also the trickiest navigationally so, if you have them,it may be prudent to take both if conditions are likely to be bad.

Terrain and Navigational Difficulties: Off roads the terrain is partly high heather and soggy bog but the higher ground offers easy dry walking. There are few navigational difficulties but take care on the transition from mountain to track after climbing Thur.

Route: Take the side road east through rolling country, ignore the turn left but a few minutes later, where the main track swings right continue straight ahead on the right-most of two minor tracks, thus heading south-east.

This minor track, never of much use finally fades out after a short distance leaving a toilsome trudge to the summit of Thur. On this stretch you may reflect that it could be worse - in fact if you have elected to do the whole route you will find that the bogland at the end certainly will be worse so .... courage!

Thur (442m/1425ft, *Tor*, steeple, tower *or* (!) bush) has a group of horizontal slabs of rocks on its indeterminate summit. The views, confined to bogland thus far, open up to reveal a wide vista of lake and mountain. This fine scenery continues on the next stretch south-east along the edge of the steep ground fronting Upper Lough Macnean. Here you will pass a region of short heather in which rock slabs seem to be arranged in such a skilful fashion that the whole effect is reminiscent of a sculpture park.

Past this area take a definite spur running east (a hint: do not go as far as a small dense clump of coniferous trees set in bogland) to nearly to its end, veering left off it here to reach a track as it emerges from forest. Turn right onto it and follow it to a minor road where your transport will be waiting if you are on the short option.

If not, turn left and walk for about 3km/2miles passing Sean McDermott's house[1] about half way along. Just after a steep descent, a turn right and a prominent bridge (in that order and in quick succession) take a left turn off this minor road onto an even more minor road. Where, after a short distance, this road swings at right-angles right and then at right-angles left, keep straight ahead onto a muddy track rather than taking the second of these bends.

Walk this track, and the path beyond it to its end in a quagmire of mud. Continue upwards through rough, broken and boggy ground with forest on the right to a track near the far corner of the forest (this track is not shown on the map). Turn left onto it and right at the nearby junction to reach the start.

Note.

1 Sean McDermott was one of the signatories of the 1916 rebellion and was executed after the rising. Whatever one's views on these events the thatched cottage and its outbuildings, furnished in the style prevalent around here in the era of McDermott's youth, are well worth a visit.

Walk 27   Benbulbin Plateau

"......I climbed Ben Bulben's back
And had the livelong Summer day to spend"

(The Tower)

Benbulbin, almost the symbol of the whole Sligo region and by far its best-known mountain presents a formidable aspect from the nearby lowlands, stern vertically-furrowed cliffs above steeply sloping grass. Surprisingly, its summit plateau is quite mundane with only occasional opportunities to view the famous cliffscape. The gullies which rend these cliffs are another matter, and they form passages to and from the plateau which are the most exciting features of the walk.

Walking Time: Distance 13km/8miles, climb 510m/1700ft, walking time 4 hrs 30 mins. A short-cut taking in only the gullies and the cliff between them reduces the distance to 5km/3miles, the climb to 340m/1100ft and the walking time to 2 hrs.

Transport: Start at GR 715424 on the minor road that runs along the south-ern side of the Benbulbin Plateau, as described under route 25. There is a frequent bus service between Sligo and Rathcormack, which will leave you within strik-ing distance of the start. Alternatively the table 282 bus might be used if your base is east of Glencar.

Map: 1:50000 sheet 16.

Terrain and Navigational Difficulties: Nearly all pathless but generally the terrain is not difficult to traverse. Care should be taken on the cliff edge between the two gullies. Take care not to lose height on the plateau in areas where there is no cliff to warn of this.

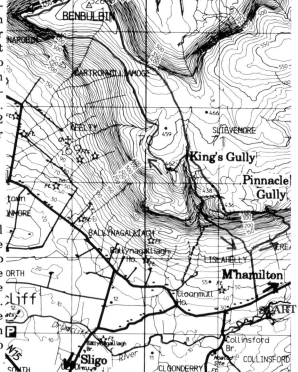

Route: Two prominent gullies are cut into the cliff: Pinnacle Gully off to your right, King's Gully to the left and the first and most difficult task is to ascend the former.

Take the track to the left of the guest house to its end at a deserted house and continue upwards through rushy fields towards steeper ground below the cliffs. Once into open land turn right and follow the enclosed land boundary, an intermittent stone wall, as far as a stream and stone chute issuing from Pinnacle Gully (this is an up and down progress, but the ground on the left is too steep to walk across with ease).

Just beyond this stream look out for a grassy track which seems to offer an easy way to the mouth of the gully. And so it does - for a while. But its target is to out-flank the cliffs so you must choose a point to leave it and head diagonally left upwards into the mouth of Pinnacle Gully, where a detached pillar of the cliffs on the gully's left gives it its appropriate name. This ascent incidentally is the most vertigo-inducing of the day, in spite of the increasingly sinister look of the gully above.

At the mouth of the gully cross a fence and climb over boulders for a few metres. Here enter a narrow, dark, steeply sloping passage on the left, a passage bounded by towering cliffs. Although this passage has more than a touch of Death Gulch about it, an impression disconcertingly heightened by the sheeps' skeletons littering the boulders which form its floor, it is quite safe and vertigo-free. Clamber to the end of the passage, turn left and scramble up the gigantic rock steps towards the light high above. Here you will find yourself on a steep grassy slope facing out over Glencar. Turn round and climb the few metres to the plateau.

The walk from here round to Benbulbin and thence to the descent gully, King's, is easily described. Keeping the upper set of cliffs on the left walk round the head of King's Gully and climb the tiny gently sloping plateau to its west, King's Mountain (462m/1527ft). It is perched high on the rim of uplands,so the views are excellent. As the area is rather dull and featureless a compass bearing may be advisable even in clear weather to reach the next target, the cliffs running east-west south of Benbulbin. Follow the cliffs round, detouring prudently here and there round the heads of massive gullies which give occasional sights of the eroded limestone pillars topping the cliff's edge.

Benbulbin (526m/1730ft, *Beann Ghulban*, Gulban's Peak or Beak Pinnacle) is marked by a trig pillar set back a little from the cliffs: there is little point in trying to find it. Beyond it continue to follow the cliffs[1] which sweep round to reveal the mirror-image cliffs of Benwiskin. Still with the cliffs on the left climb a grassy mound and beyond it head directly towards King's Mountain, from here a prominent tilted plateau.

Near King's Mountain descend along King's Gully to pick up a path which runs increasingly higher above the gully's left side (but only because the gully cuts increasingly lower). This path joins a grassy track whose predominant direction is east towards Glencar Lough, though it doesn't matter too much if you lose it. The track fades away near a stone wall – the one alongside which you ascended earlier in the day. Turn right on the far side of this wall and walk to the start.

Notes.

1. Some rare plants grow here in crevices on the limestone cliffs, (especially these north-facing ones) and among the scree, in locations so inaccessible that they are protected from sheep (and humans). Among these limestone-loving alpine plants are the fringed sandwort which grows nowhere else in Ireland, mountain avens, mountain sorrel, least willow and purple saxifrage. These cliffs were above the glacial level during the last ice age, and the plants survived the tundra-like conditions and thrive here to this day.

Walk 28   Glenade: Eagle's Rock

The eastern side of the Benbulbin Plateau facing Glenade boasts a strange rock formation: a huge column of limestone, Eagle's Rock, has detached itself from the plateau and, with several subsidiary columns, rises sheer, forbidding and overpowering, some tens of metres from the main cliffs[1]. Two variations are given: both traverse the eerie passage between cliff and column, the short one then descending through pleasant woodland back to the road, the longer ascending to the plateau before reaching the road at Glenade Lough.

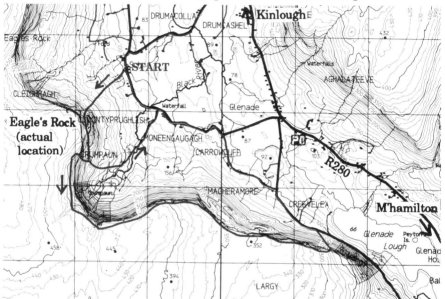

Walking Time: Distance 10.5km/6.5miles, climb 420m/1400ft, walking time 3 hrs 30 mins for the long variation. Distance 3.5km/2miles, climb 420m/1400ft, walking time 1 hr 30 mins for the short variation.

Transport: Car to Glenade (at GR 787486). From the north take the R280 south of Largydonnell. Pass the church on the left, take the next turn right, drive for 1.3 miles to a tee, turn left and park 0.1 miles further on at a cottage and laneway on the right.

From the south take the R280 for about 2 miles beyond the end of Glenade Lough taking a left turn here. This is the turn right of the previous paragraph.

The table 291 bus service might be used to get to and from Park Cross (GR 796528).

Map: 1:50000 sheet 16. Both this map and the half-inch map place Eagle's Rock about 1.5km/1mile north of its actual location.

Terrain and Navigational Difficulties: Mostly pathless terrain (apart from roads) but not too difficult except for some boulder hopping at Eagle's Rock. At the far side of the Rock watch out for the transition to the homeward route for the short variation or to the plateau for the long. The descent from the plateau is quite easy to find but ensure that you don't miss it. Generally navigation is not over-difficult.

Route: Take the laneway, cross left over the first gate and the fence beyond it (carefully please!) and keep this fence on the right directly towards Eagle's Rock. Its profile changes uncannily: from some angles blending innocuously into the plateau, from others a skyscraper clearly detached from it. From near the start of the walk it looks quite mundane...but wait!

At the top of the initial fence cross a second to face into the defile between Eagle's Rock and the cliffs of the plateau edge, a defile which has an almost pre-historic feel about it, accentuated by the impressive fossil imprints easily found among the boulders littering its steep floor. At first glance this defile appears to be a cul-de-sac for all except rock climbers and would-be suicides, but it is in fact an easy ascent, though you should beware of wobbly rocks underfoot.

Descend from the top of the defile into a narrow valley between steep partly wooded ground on the right, and crumbling subsidiary columns succeeded by a hummocky grassy ridge on the left. Along here, whether car- or plateau-bound a little care is needed to find a ruin (the only one hereabouts) and from there a path at a stone pen just beyond it.

For the *short* route turn left onto the path and walk downhill, forest on the right to reach abandoned farm buildings. Take the gradually improving path/track here to tarmac, turn left and walk 1km/half-mile back to the start.

For the *long* route turn right onto the path and follow it up through steep ground which avoids even steeper ground and cliffs to right and left. On the plateau navigation is easy. Walk south, cliffs on the left, cross a shallow channel where the cliffs bend left and continue along the cliff edge past some spectacular grassed rock sculpture below on the left. As you progress look back occasionally at Eagle's Rock to observe how different it appears at various angles: four columns emerging unobtrusively one after another and later merging back equally unobtrusively into the plateau.

At length and still on high ground, you come directly opposite the western (nearest) end of Glenade Lough (*Gleann Éada*, Eada's Glen). Look out here for forest climbing the hillside and about 100 metres before reaching it cross the fence on the left into rough vegetation to pick up a narrow track heading unwaveringly diagonally down to the left. At the valley floor turn left onto a narrow tarmac road.

The walk ends with 4km/2.5miles on quiet rural roads. Turn first left, walk to its end at a tee, turn left again and walk directly to the start.

Note.
1. These impressive pillars and the small but steep-sided hillocks and ridges to be seen down on the valley sides later in the walk were formed at the end of the last glacial period. You must imagine the entire glen filled by a glacier that had scooped out and deepened the pre-existing shallow river valley, making its sides almost vertical. When the climate improved and the glacier retreated the side walls, now without their glacial supports, slumped forward from the cliffs towards the valley floor. These formations may be seen both here and in Glencar, notably in Swiss Valley (Walks 15 and 25).

Walk 29   Dartry Hills: Keeloges

The approach to Keeloges from Glenade in some ways mirrors the approach to the Benbulbin Plateau from Glencar: in both cases a scenic valley is overlooked by limestone cliffscapes topped by rolling plateau. Unlike Glencar however, the ascent of the intimidating looking Keelogues cliffs presents no problems as it is on an easy track. A short but exciting ascent with good views leading to a tramp across lonely and austere moorland, punctuated by occasional lakes.

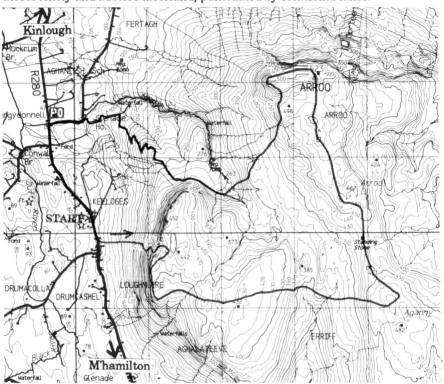

Walking Time: Distance 13.5km/8.5miles, climb 610m/2000ft, time 4 hrs 45 mins.

Transport: From the north (Bundoran) take the R280 to less than a mile south of the village of Largydonnell parking near the church on the left at GR 803502.

From the south (Manorhamilton) take the R280, drive past Glenade Lough and park at the church on the right just over 2 miles beyond it. Depending on your base, the infrequent timetable 291 bus which serves Park (GR 797528) might be used.

Map: 1:50000 sheet 16.

Terrain and Navigational Difficulties: Tracks and road at the beginning and end, otherwise pathless. The moorland above may be a trifle intimidating but the lakes are good navigational aids and it is easy to descend over the rim of the plateau except where there are abrupt cliffs – the type easiest to avoid.

Route: Walk south along the R280 for about 400m, crossing here the wooden gate on the left (if you walk as far as the shop selling handknits you have gone about 200m too far). As you ascend directly beyond the gate you will see the great cliff of Keeloges ahead, relenting at one section into a steep grassy slope. At this section a great gash runs down the slope and on the right of it is a zig-zag track. It is this track which is the first target.

Climb up the track and once on the plateau walk to the oval-shaped Keeloges Lough (GR 813498). This lies just to the south of Keeloges mountain and is distinguishable by the tiny beaches of coarse-grained sand at each end. Since it is the only lake anywhere near it is hardly necessary to mention this distinguishing mark.

Having toiled up to the plateau it is little extra effort to explore it. From the lough follow the cliffs southwards. Where the land begins to drop significantly head direction on a compass bearing to Lough Aganny passing on the way a marsh surrounded by fencing, a reassuring landmark though not essential to find, and then the headwaters of two streams.

From the well-built cairn just north of Lough Aganny the route north along the high ground at the centre of the plateau is simply described. Pass the standing stone[1] just to the left of the direct route, walk along the left side of Lough Arroo and from the cairn on its north side head directly to the trig pillar on Arroo (523m/1720ft), perched on the edge of cliffs and so with excellent views out towards Donegal Bay and Slieve League beyond.

Continue along the cliff edge west so keeping it on the right, and then swing left (south) with it into lower ground, making sure to avoid the numerous swallow holes[2] in the high heather and boggy ground.

At length you will descend to a valley which has a bog track wending its way down through it. Turn right onto this track and follow it down to a minor road. Continue straight ahead downhill here. At the R280 turn left and walk the 1.5km/1mile to the start.

Notes.

1. A note on standing stones appears under walk 30.
2. The origin of the swallow holes scattered like bomb craters hereabouts is interesting. Think of a layer of a rock such as shale overlying a greater expanse of limestone. Rain water falling on the shale keep to the surface but when the resultant streams eventually reach its edge they work a passage vertically down through the highly soluble limestone and disappear underground. So a swallow hole is eventually formed. Now suppose the edge of the shale is eroded so that there is a new border between it and the underlying limestone. The stream abandons the original swallow hole and forms a new one. Hence the seemingly randomly scattered swallow holes in this and other areas where other rocks overlie limestone.
   Some swallow holes shelter a luxuriant vegetation including low trees, whose tops are stunted as soon as they rise above the level of the hole and so face the full force of the wind.

Walk 30   Central Dartry Hills

The wedge of mountain between Glenade and Lough Melvin is predominantly a rolling moorland, sizeable but not very lofty. The moorland's edges are much more distinctive: cliffs north and west and, facing out over Lough Melvin a strange area of tiny hillocks snuggled below the cliffs of the plateau. Two options are given: a short walk to these hillocks with a return directly along the plateau edge or a much longer walk also taking in the hillocks as well as much of the plateau above.

Walking Time: Distance 4km/2.5 miles, climb 160m/500ft, walking time 1hr 30 mins for the short walk. Distance 10km/6.5miles, climb 400m/1300ft, walking 3 hrs 30 mins for the long.

Transport: From Kinlough take the R281 turning second right after 2.8 miles. Drive uphill for a further 1.3 miles to park at a bog road on the right just before a bridge (at GR 858516).

From Manorhamilton take the R282 to Rossinver, turn left here into Glenaniff and drive for a further 5.6 miles to park at the second of two adjacent bog roads on the left.

This walk or a variation of it descending into Glenade (it can easily be combined with route 29) might be done using the table 291 bus .

Map: 1:50000 sheet 16.

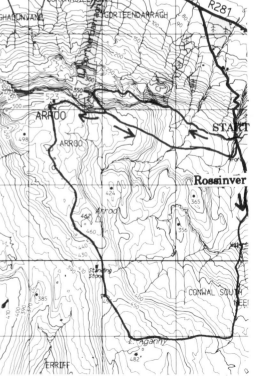

Terrain and Navigational Difficulties: A few stretches of bog road, otherwise pathless with some difficult terrain as well as much easy walking. Compass bearings are essential on the plateau though with many clear and long breaks in the cliffs of the plateau's edge, even in the worst conditions a direct descent to *somewhere* is nearly always possible.

Route: Take the bog road, which runs south for a few metres and then resolutely west. It terminates after about five minutes steady walking; continue on roughly straight ahead keeping to the same height to cross two tiny streams. Beyond these is a forestry plantation wedged closely against steeply rising ground left. Walk with the plantation on the right thus revealing a cluster of 'Alpine peaks', eight in all rising impressively ahead[1].

Impressive but tiny. The soaring 'peaks', flanked by rocky cliffs and steep slopes are dwarfed by the edge of the plateau behind them and the sheep grazing the slopes put the scene into perspective: the 'peaks' are hillocks no more than 30m/100ft high. Walk to the far end of the hillocks and climb to a stone wall which threads high up between the last two. Follow it left to reach a path heading away from the cliffs of the plateau edge and giving easy access to this edge.[2]

Here a decision. You can take the shorter walk which returns directly from here or the longer one which explores the plateau. For the *short* walk keep the plateau edge somewhere on the left (the exact distance is not critical) and walk, watching out for swallow holes in the high heather, to reach either the end of the bog road on which you started or a little more adventurously, one farther south if you keep a little further away from the plateau's edge.

For the *long* walk turn west to follow the cliffs on the right, so revealing an impressive coastline north and a scarpland to the west. At the trig pillar on Arroo (523m/1712ft), head directly south, at first steeply down over patches of limestone chips, to the well-built cairn directly north of Arroo Lough, an Australia-shaped lake. From the lake continue south along the plateau, passing a standing stone[3] on the right to reach another well-built cairn just north of Lough Aganny, beyond which yet another cairn may be seen (but need not be attained).

From the cairn head directly east to the headwaters of the first north-flowing tributary, 1km/half-mile away. Turn left to follow a fence which allows access to the tributary's bank only near its junction with the main stream. This access is worth waiting for as the bank here is a delightful spot for a snack. Near a secluded and lovely waterfall cross the main stream (careful, the rocks are slippery) and ascend the steep bank opposite to reach a bog road. Take it to tarmac and the start.

Notes.

1. The origin of these hillocks is outlined under Walk 28.

2. Much of this whole area seems to be typical of the area described long ago by Fynes Moryson (1566-1617): *"the land is uneven, mountainous, soft, watery, woody, and open to winds and floods of rain, and so fenny, as it hath bogs upon the very tops of the mountains, not bearing man or beast, but dangerous to pass ..."* Don't worry about the last comment!

3. Standing stones could belong to any of a wide range of eras and if they are in lines may have been used in the study of celestial bodies or to form a boundary of some sort. This isolated example may have been a tombstone: all these explanations are no more than conjecture.

Castlegal Range West

"He slept under the hill of Lugnagall[1]
And might have known at last unhaunted sleep
Under that cold and vapour turbaned steep"

(The Man who Dreamed of Faeryland)

The general rule about the higher ground in the west of the region is that the edges are of more interest than the centre. The splendid exception to this is the Castlegal Range, the mountains between Glencar and Lough Gill. A range of no great height (it reaches 463m/1519ft), it has nonetheless a complex array of clustered flat-topped hills ringed by low cliffs, and high passes flanked by steep rises. This walk takes in the western end of the range and gives excellent views over Lough Gill to the south and the Benbulbin Plateau to the north.

Walking Time: Distance 12km/7.5miles and climb 590m/1950ft for the full walk, that is using only one car. This, allowing 15 mins extra time for one steep descent, should take 4 hrs 15 mins walking time. However, a second car may be left at the junction of the N16 and the Glackbaun road (as described below) thus reducing the distance to 10km/6.5miles and the time to less than 4 hrs. This time may of course be further reduced by driving the second car along the increasingly narrow Glackbaun road.

Transport: Car to GR 719411 on the N16. From Sligo take the N16 for about 3 miles, watching out here for a black-on-yellow diamond-shaped road sign indicating that the main road turns right with a side road continuing straight ahead. Park carefully at the side road on the left 1.2 miles farther on. If coming west along the N16 look for the brown sign 'Glencar Lake 2k' and park at the side road right 0.4 miles farther on.

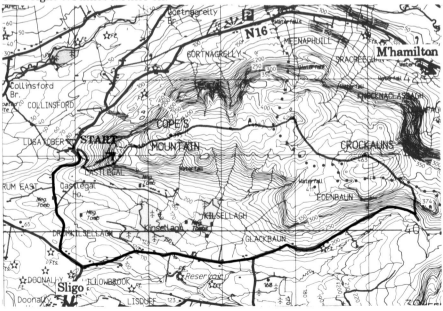

As outlined above a second car may be left at the junction of the Glackbaun road thus avoiding a trudge along the N16, usually a busy road, at the end of the walk. Drive back towards Sligo, parking at the left turn after 1.3 miles.

If travelling by bus you could use the Monday to Friday table 282 service. The 'Glencar Lake 2k' sign gives ample warning to alight. In this case a better finish to catch the bus would be north to the N16, that is the reverse of the start of walk 32.

The walk may be combined with Walks 32 and 21 to give a long walk along the entire range. This means a bus to the start as described in the previous paragraph or two cars, one to be left at the starting point of Walk 21.

Map: 1:50000 sheet 16.

Terrain and Navigational Difficulties: Nearly the whole length is pathless except for the road walk at the end. With a bewildering array of small peaks and low cliffs in the high ground of the range this can be a rather intimidating area in bad visibility. In these conditions the best plan is to head relentlessly east, diverting round obstacles until the descent into Glackbaun with its road and fairly prominent isolated house at about GR 771402 materialise. In bad weather not an area for the faint-hearted or the inexperienced.

Route: Cross the gate supported on concrete pillars opposite the side road, and walk uphill to the top of the *first* field beyond it to reach a wide but secluded grassy track, difficult to discern at this point. Turn right onto it, thus advancing steadily upwards through scattered trees. It turns left at a fence and where it turns left again (and here you are at a grassy rib heading uncompromisingly upwards), leave the track and ascend directly, the fence on the right. Near the top, cross another fence which weaves among rocky outcrops and walk the short distance to Cope's Mountain (west top) (331m/1056ft) which has a small cairn.

Walking east from the west top[1] cross a narrow grassy plain to enter an area of limestone knolls bounded on the north by cliffs and rotting rocky pinnacles overlooking Glencar. The exact route here is immaterial as long as you continue roughly east, but a more northerly route closer to Glencar offers an intermittent path and dramatic cliffscapes.

Beyond this area contour round a broad grassy gully which falls towards the western end of Glencar Lough. Here the terrain is wet and flatter with occasional small depressions, though the more distant scenery is just as splendid.

This stretch ends in a distinct descent into lower ground beyond which watch out for a wall ascending the right flank of Crockauns (463m/1527ft, *Crocaun,* little hill) ahead. Ascend beside it and where it levels off and peters out in hummocky ground strike off left directly towards the top. (A word of warning: the initial wall is clear enough in good weather but there are several walls in the area so in bad visibility do not follow a wall without checking direction.)

Crockauns has a well-built cairn and commands lovely views, that towards the Benbulbin Plateau to the north being particularly noteworthy. As you gradually descend east from Crockauns, keep to the high ground and watch out for two high grassy hills. Aim for the right side of the more southerly, perhaps encountering a wall-junction as you near it. (Note: if you are on the combined route walk *between*

The Doons

these two hills so descending steeply into the highest point of the next pass.)
Make a steep descent right close to hawthorn bushes into Glackbaun. At the foot
of the descent turn right onto a very narrow road, just wide enough for one car.
There follows a scenic stretch of 5km/3miles to the N16, below the steep ground
and cliffs of Castlegal. If you have not left transport at the junction of the N16
walk the extra 2km/1.3miles to the start.

Notes.

The 19th century cleric, Fr.O'Rorke, didn't think all that much of the Castlegal Range. He
writes: *"Between Coolageboy* [ie Keelogyboy] *and Benbulben intervenes Cashel Gal or* Slieve-
gan-báiste *mountains, a fine bold range, which would be more thought of if found elsewhere,
but which suffers from its neighbourhood with the beautiful Benbulbin"*.

The old spelling *'Cashel Gal'* is more faithful to the pronunciation of the name of the range
than the standard present-day spelling 'Castlegal'. Notice also the varied spelling of place
names in this area, even within the one sentence. *'Slieve-gan-báiste'* means 'mountains
without rain', a flattering though unfortunately inaccurate appellation. The alternative
translation of the name 'the mountain without baptism' doesn't seem to make much sense.

1. Lugnagull is a townland in Glencar at the foot of Cope's Mountain but from the poem it
   appears to be a mountain.

2. Along this path to the east of Cope's Mountain, Sir Frederick Hamilton is said to have
   met a sorry end in 1641. With some of his horsemen, he was returning home in the dark
   after raiding Sligo Town (it is not clear why he chose such an inconvenient and
   hazardous route). He forced a local shepherd to guide him and he, understandably not
   well-disposed towards Sir Frederick or his plundering, misdirected the horsemen over
   the cliffs. Since then this place has been known as Hamilton's Leap. Yeats used this
   story in his tale 'The Curse of the Fires and of the Shadows'.

66

Walk 32   Castlegal Range East

Like the western, the eastern half of the Castlegal Range stretching from Keelogyboy to Leean, is a region of rugged hills, but here the individual peaks are much more distinct and are separated from each other by closely spaced passes, so that each peak is prefaced by a steep climb and followed by a steep descent. The cliffs, low but difficult to negotiate, may cause unexpected detours and complicate otherwise simple navigation. Views are excellent throughout.

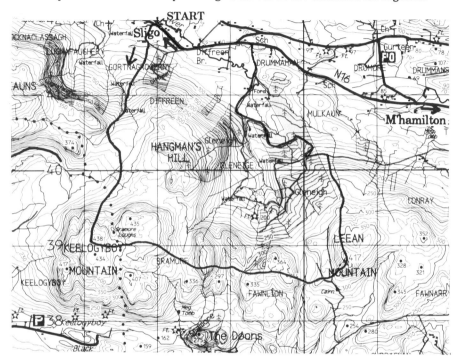

Walking Time: Distance 13km/8miles, climb 650m/2100ft, walking time 5 hrs 45 mins allowing 45 mins extra for a few steep descents and bad vegetation.

Transport: Drive to the side road off the northern side of the N16 about 1.5 miles east of the eastern end of Glencar Lough (GR 781419). The side road is signposted 'Glencar Lake'.

The table 282 bus service might be used for this walk.

Map: The whole route is covered on 1:50000 sheet 16 and all but the start and end on sheet 25 which will therefore just about do.

Terrain and Navigational Difficulties: Few stretches of track and some quite difficult underfoot conditions. Navigationally the start is easy but the area around Keelogyboy has quite complicated terrain and a resolute compass bearing roughly east with a prudent veering round obstacles may be necessary in poor visibility. The second half of the route (that is from the forest plantation on) is straightforward.

Route: Walk west along the N16 (that is towards Sligo) turning left through a gate after a few metres. Walk up the track beyond it and where it swings at right angles left to a farmhouse continue straight ahead through wet rushy fields, so heading for a small copse straddling a high river valley.

Keep the copse on the right and at its top pick up a track which keeps close to the steep ground near Crockauns to the west. At the top of the pass the track fades in high flat bogland. Here choose a good point to head south to Keelogyboy, picking a route which gains high (and drier) ground quickly. Keelogyboy's top (438m/1450ft) is a rather confusing quasi-plateau of humps and hollows. Here a limestone field, a series of stone ridges aligned roughly north-south, is a useful indicator of the proximity of the top, which is marked by several cairns all at about the same level. From the plateau drop east to the next pass, the one facing Sramore. Ascend Sramore near a fence which has resulted in heather right and grass left of it: sheep must be grazing only on the left.

This steep, arduous climb to Sramore (about 410m/1350ft) is merely a prelude to an even steeper, more arduous descent east around rocky outcrops and a jungle of high shrubs. On this descent watch out ahead for a forest to the left of the main ridge, with a track starting on its right side and running downhill to the right. Cross a gate to reach this track and turn left onto it to walk with a fence or wall on the left generally uphill (but with some dips). With no navigational problems this is an easy stretch allowing a confident stride.

Retribution (worse still undeserved retribution) follows. A steep punishing descent ensues to another pass where turf is being cut. Cross this and the rocky ground beyond it to reach a grassy track traversing the second installment of the pass. From here climb directly to Leean (417m/1373ft) whose trig pillar dispels any remaining doubt you may have had about your position (if there's no trig pillar it will, alas greatly intensify this doubt).

The descent from Leean is roughly north, thus heading towards a church across upper Glencar. If you keep forest a little way off on your left you can reach a side road using gates and without climbing fences. Turn left onto the side road, turn right at the crossroads and take the forest track (later a side road) back to the N16. Turn left onto it and walk less than 1.5km/1mile back to the start.

Walk 33   Gleniff Horseshoe

A high-level circuit commanding wide views over sea, littoral and mountains. It starts with a heart-thumping, very steep but grassy ascent to Benwiskin, followed by a long exhilarating level stretch which ends in an emotional and physical dip at the head of Gleniff. It ends with a memorable finish after another scenic high-level section to Tievebaun. A long and varied round.

Walking Time: Distance 16.5km/10.5miles, climb 950m/3100ft, walking time 6 hrs. The miners' road may be used as a convenient escape route at about the half way point.

Transport: By car to Ballaghnatrillick (GR 737502), a small village 15km/10miles north-east of Sligo (by crow-flight). A road map might be helpful to find it. An A to B variation may be done using the bus (see below).

Map: 1:50000 sheet 16.

Terrain and Navigational Difficulties: Nearly all pathless ground but usually quite firm and so it is easy to make good progress. Navigationally take a modicum of care and in good weather at least the terrain will guide you. The only difficult area, underfoot and navigationally, is the low ground at the head of the valley.

Route: Before starting take a look at Benwiskin to the south-west, as you will not see it as strikingly from any other point. To the left a smooth steep grassy profile ends in a wavering line at the top of the summit cliffs, and these plunge to the north in partly overhanging, wicked precipices. A memorable sight.

Take the westerly of the two roads south-east into Gleniff (the one *not* signposted 'Yeats Country Drive') and walk about 1km/half-mile to where forest starts on the right. Take the driveway here towards the house set back from the road, climb the steps on the left just before it and walk up the firebreak through encompassing conifers, a route which avoids the fences of a more direct approach, though it postpones the views except for the occasional glimpse of steep-sided Benwiskin directly ahead.

The far end of the plantation (it is shown on the 1:50000 map rising much higher on the flank of Benwiskin than it actually does) marks the start of the steep ascent indicated in the introduction, and this ascent is prefaced by a short cliff face which may be avoided by contouring left. Climb the slope beyond, which might appear to be well-nigh vertical but which a tedious mathematical calculation reveals to be hardly more than 35 or 40 degrees. At the top of Benwiskin (514m/1702ft), more a cliff edge than a true summit turn left, so that the cliffs are on the right, and enjoy the unusual sight of long views on both sides with the great sweep of high ground to the east revealing the full circuit to be walked.

Navigation from here on as far as the head of the valley is easy, the fence on the left for part of the way being almost unnecessary for navigational purposes. Climb the short distance to point 508m/1675ft beyond which seemingly undeviating progress is halted by a great amphitheatre gouged out of the cliffs and surrounded by stacks of horizontal slabs, some reminiscent of tottering piles of dishes.

Continue on round this obstacle to the head of the valley, cross the miners' road[1] near a gate on it and climb gently with a fence on the left and later an electricity line on the right to the TV road which ends at Truskmore. You might surmise that all these manifestations of modernity are not compatible with wilderness and beauty and you would be right.

Walk to the mast at the top of Truskmore (647m/2120ft) cutting corners on the road as long as you are sure that you will be able to find it again. At the summit the vast morass of dreary moorland stretching away south-east[2] is much in evidence, though the onward stretch looks more promising.

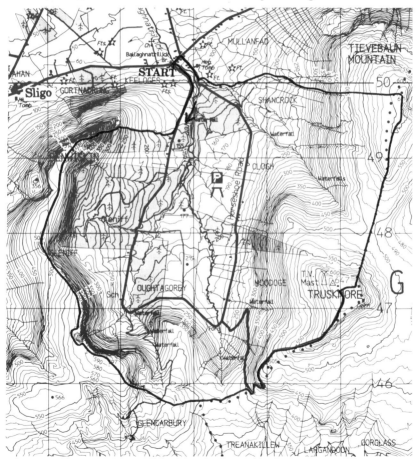

Indeed scenery improves greatly after Truskmore. Walk to a shelter 200 metres or so east of the TV mast and descend through square-cut boulders to the pass facing Tievebaun, following a wall and later a ditch on the county boundary between Sligo (left) and Leitrim (right). The wall resumes at steeper ground near the summit and where it heads left downhill, pick up a fence going straight ahead gently uphill. This fence in turn swings downhill but here the summit cairn is only 50 metres or so to the east of the corner. From the summit of Tievebaun (611m/1720ft) the views of the cliffs across Glenade are particularly impressive.

Retrace steps to the corner and descend following the fence. Some way down, where there is a patch of steep slag-like scree, walk along a burgeoning stream on the left. The rule now is to keep this stream 'somewhere' within reach on the left until you reach the road. In detail: as you descend watch out for a farm on the opposite bank and walk the short distance down towards it and then down the track near it: where it unexpectedly peters out after a few metres, walk diagonally left downhill across a field and cross a stile. Take a bridge across the stream to reach tarmac and turn right for the village.

Bus Alternative: The table 291 service goes to Ballaghnatrillick from Bundoran on **Saturday** mornings only and depending on your base might be useful. Alternatively, a frequent bus to Creevykeel Crossroads on the N15 leave a walk of 5km/3miles to Ballaghnatrillick.

If travelling by bus a walk ending at Rathcormack may be undertaken. Keep to the route as described above as far as the amphitheatre, walk along the top of the cliffs around the valley to the south-west of Benwiskin as far as Benbulbin and, as described in Walk 27, descend via King's Gully. Once on the road head to Rathcormack from where there is a good bus service.

The total distance for this walk is 15km/9.5miles from Ballaghnatrillick to Rathcormack, the climb is 560/185, the walking time 5 hrs.

Notes.

1. A lode of barytes, a soft heavy mineral which comes in a variety of colours, runs right through the mountains from the head of Gleniff in the north, to Tormore overlooking Glencar in the south. The lode had a maximum depth of 3m/10ft. Formerly used in the production of paint, its most widespread application now is as part of a lubricant for drills used in offshore oil exploration.

   Mining began in the late 19th century and has continued sporadically since, never with conspicuous success. No mining has taken place here since 1979. The ore has been transported at various times northwards and southwards towards Gleniff and Glencar respectively as the evidence of aerial cableways suggests.

   A railway to service these mines once ran along the western side of Gleniff. The purpose of this short-lived narrow gauge (2ft) line was to transport barytes from the mines at the high ground to the south. The mineral was first transported down the mountain on two other narrow-gauge lines to the head of the valley. The 2ft gauge line then transported the barytes along Gleniff, through Ballaghnatrillick and thence to the small port of Mullaghmore about 11km/7miles away. Work on the railway commenced in 1928 with a great burst of enthusiasm. Sadly the line had closed by 1931, by which time only the section from the head of the valley to Ballaghnatrillick had been used to any extent.

2. On the gently sloping plateau south-east of here lie extensive sites, evidence of neolithic people who lived there 5000 years ago. The sites cover an area of 12sq km/5sq miles and consist of small clusters of houses in five 'villages', (one with as many as 20 houses), an impressive network of field boundaries, cairns and wedge tombs.

The sites must have been overwhelmed by the advance of bog which in turn is now being eroded by over-grazing by sheep, thus exposing parts of the sites once again. The area is at present being excavated.